THE NEW
HOME
BOOK

THE NEW
HOME BOOK

DESIGNING AND TRANSFORMING
YOUR LIVING SPACE

ELIZABETH WILHIDE

TIME
LIFE
BOOKS

This book was conceived and produced by
Breslich & Foss Ltd
20 Wells Mews
London W1T 3HQ

Jacket photograph: Paul Ryan/International Interiors
    (Designer: Elaine Goff)

Printed in China.

CONTENTS

INTRODUCTION

Designing and decorating a home of your own can be one of the most satisfying things you ever do. It can also be one of the most daunting. Most of us have a mental picture of our dream house, but when we look around at our own four walls, we despair of ever bridging the gap. *The New Home Book* is specially designed to help you to turn those dreams into reality, whether you have just moved to a new home and are wondering what to tackle first, or simply wish to revamp a single area.

All dream houses have one thing in common: they fit like a glove. They are not only tailor-made to individual lifestyles so that they function properly, but they also express personal tastes and innermost desires. Your dream home will be the one that suits the way you live, that surrounds you with the colours and patterns you like and provides a sense of welcome every time you step through the door.

How do you get there? Some people seem to be born with an instinct for what they like and experience no difficulty at all in heading straight for it. For the rest of us, it takes a certain amount of creative daydreaming, careful planning and a solid grounding in all the practicalities. This is where *The New Home Book* comes in. It offers sources of inspiration, practical know-how and decorators'

tips: the essential background for creating a decorative scheme in your own personal style.

Principally arranged room by room, *The New Home Book* is designed to be used alongside a notebook. This is the place in which to note the answers to the Assessment Checklist on pages 14–15 and to draw up your plan of action. Use it to keep an on-going record of your preferences and to record specific details, sources of materials, prices and measurements. With the notebook, you can keep track of useful addresses and phone numbers, product specifications and costs.

You will also find it helpful to have some clear plastic wallets. These will help you to organise colour swatches, fabric samples and magazine clippings in an accessible way. Once you have built up a personal collection of reference material, it's easy to mix and match colours and patterns for the perfect decorative scheme.

On pages 174–79 you will find graph paper and templates with which to make sketch plans of every area in your home, plan furniture layouts and experiment with different arrangements.

From daydreaming to sourcing and getting the job done, *The New Home Book* will accompany you every step of the way.

To achieve the perfect home, you have to know your own tastes and preferences. Home improvement schemes vary widely in levels of complexity, from simple redecoration and furnishing, to more ambitious projects that involve spatial change. But they all require careful planning in order to achieve a successful result.

KNOW WHAT YOU LIKE

Whether you intend to do all the work yourself, or plan to hire a professional decorator, the essential first step is to know what you like. For many people, this stage in the proceedings is the fun part, the chance to let the imagination run riot, regardless of the usual constraints of time and budget. For others, particularly those who find themselves overwhelmed by the immense variety of options portrayed in the media and for sale in the shops, uncovering their true preferences can involve a little more soul-searching.

The time you take to indulge in a little creative daydreaming is time well spent. Decorating mistakes happen for many reasons, but one of the most common is setting out without a clear idea of what it is you are after. If you don't consider your own responses to different decorative ideas, you are much more likely to succumb to a too-hasty decision that you regret later. Taking the trouble to think hard about what you like will ultimately make all the difference between coming up with a well-considered and sympathetic scheme and adopting a potentially disastrous scattered approach.

Think of this exercise as a way of formulating a brief. If you were to employ an interior designer or architect, he or she would want to know something about you: the hobbies and activities you enjoy, the decorative styles that appeal to you, the colours you adore and those you loathe.

Collect images that catch your eye: postcards of places or paintings, pictures of flowers, food or fashion, snaps of treasured belongings. Focus on shapes and colours, patterns and textures. Don't worry if the images you have selected have nothing to do with interior decoration. The only criterion for selection is that they must appeal to you.

However excited you are to get going, it is important not to rush the process. You may need some time to build up a useful cuttings file of ideas and you may also need to overcome a slight feeling of self-consciousness as you do so. But it is important to remember that this visual library is your point of departure. It's a creative tool that will enable you to steer a course through all the options and head off confidently in the direction that you want to take.

Later, you can begin to turn your collection into the basis of a sample board, the edited assembly of ideas that professional designers use to shape a scheme (see pages 66–67).

Not even the most talented designer can devise a scheme in a vacuum. Start by collecting appealing images and keep an eye out for common themes and patterns. You may discover that you are naturally drawn to certain colours or combinations of materials, or that your taste is surprisingly eclectic and diverse. What counts is to find out how you want to live.

▪ Make a list of your favourite things. If your house was on fire and your loved ones were safe, which of your possessions would you save?

▪ Cast your mind back to places where you felt comfortable or inspired. It might be a beachhouse, a house from your childhood, even a hotel room.

▪ What colours, patterns and textures attract you? Take a peek inside your wardrobe and pull out the clothes you love. What do they have in common?

▪ Make a list of your favourite stores. Do you like to rummage in antiques shops, or do you make a beeline for the designer homeware department?

PLANNING
FOR
ACTION

ANALYSE
YOUR HOME

Impulse has a very real part to play in any creative endeavour and home decoration is no exception. But, dull as it may sound, advance planning and preparation more often than not save the day. One of the functions of the Notebook is to serve as a place where you can note preliminary observations. As you move from area to area in your home, write down obvious problems and defects, along with possible remedies. You should also include existing features that might need to be enhanced. At the same time, you should be thinking about your home as a whole: problems with related areas may indicate the need for better spatial planning or even structural change.

▶ NOTEBOOK

It can be difficult to gain an objective view of one's own surroundings. Once you have lived somewhere for a while, it's hard to see it as others do – given time and familiarity, minor defects such as the chipped paint on the landing, the cluttered corner of the living room, the broken kitchen drawer simply fade into the background until they become almost invisible. On the other hand, if you have just moved to a new home, absolutely everything will be unfamiliar and this very strangeness may well conceal underlying problems.

In the first instance, the answer can be to exploit those moments when the scales fall from your eyes and you see your home in a new and often not very flattering light. These often tend to occur when you have been away for a time. Everyone knows the feeling: you walk in through the door and what you have long overlooked hits you right in the face. The kitchen could do with a fresh coat of paint, the

Part of the process of analysing your home is to take a look at the way you move through it (LEFT). 'Circulation space', or halls, stairs and landings, should offer clear, unobstructed routes from area to area. Work sequences are another important aspect to consider (RIGHT). How easy or difficult is it to perform certain routine tasks?

curtains in the dining room are past their sell-by-date, the bedroom is a disorganised mess.

You can also experience the same critical awareness when someone visits your home for the first time. Suddenly, those battered floorboards are embarrassingly obvious. To make a proper assessment of your home when you are thoroughly familiar with it, you need to think yourself into that same frame of mind.

Uncovering the hidden assets and defects of a new home requires the opposite strategy. You need to experience a space under different conditions before potential problems emerge. A poorly planned kitchen will reveal its true colours only when you have unpacked the shopping and cooked several meals. Similarly, you can't begin to assess lighting requirements until you have had a chance to observe a space at different times.

ASSESSMENT CHECKLIST

Your answers to the checklist will naturally fall into two categories: those that concern the way your home is planned as a whole and those specific to certain areas. Note the answers in your Notebook.

FUNCTION

▓ Does your home serve all of your present needs? Is there space to entertain, to work quietly, somewhere for children to play safely? How does the basic arrangement of rooms accommodate your current lifestyle?

▓ Which areas feel particularly cramped? Where could you really use more space?

▓ Are there any areas that you rarely use at all?

▓ How well does each room serve its purpose?

▓ Anticipate the future. How will your home function in the years to come, when your way of living may well have changed?

▓ What improvements could be made to the way you move from space to space? Analyse main routes from room to room and within rooms.

▓ Is there enough storage space? Where does clutter always build up?

APPEARANCE

■ What do you like most about each room? What do you like the least?

■ Do the basic surfaces and finishes need decorating or updating?

■ Does the room receive good natural light? Is the existing artificial lighting adequate?

■ Which pieces of furniture would you like to replace? Which need a make-over? Which would you keep at all costs?

■ Think about spatial quality. Does the ceiling seem too low? Is the room an awkward shape?

■ Are there any essential repairs that need to be made? Note defects such as patches of damp, cracking, uneven plasterwork or loose floorboards.

SERVICES

■ Are there enough power points? Do you need new phone lines or ISDN lines?

■ Is your heating system as energy- and cost-efficient as it might be?

■ Can improvements be made to security? Window locks, for example, are simple to install.

■ Is your home easy and economical to maintain?

Assess the function or functions that each area of the home serves. This means taking a good look at what really goes on. Living rooms (LEFT) and kitchens (RIGHT) are often multi-purpose spaces, particularly in family homes.

SAFETY

If you have children, or share your home with an elderly relative or someone with special needs, you may need to consider additional safety features.

OPTIONS FOR CHANGE

Some problems demand specific solutions. If your home is in poor physical repair or you have identified a major defect, such as the presence of dry rot, rising damp or an infestation of woodworm, no amount of cosmetic tinkering with the symptoms is going to put it right. You will simply have to get at the root cause of the problem and treat it; professional assistance will generally be required in circumstances like these.

Many deficiencies fall into a kind of grey area, where more than one remedy may work. In such cases, you will need to assess your priorities and the amount of time and money you are prepared to spend on improvement. If your living room is dark and feels confined, for example, there's more than one way to approach the problem. A brighter, fresher colour scheme and better furniture arrangement might help. A more radical solution might be to choose a different room with a better aspect as the living room. More extreme still would be to change the space physically, by knocking through a partition wall, enlarging or adding windows, or building an extension.

ESSENTIAL REPAIRS

Keeping up with running repairs can prevent serious problems from developing. You may need expert advice if you spot the following symptoms:

- Leaking roofs.
- Fungal growths.
- Musty smells, patches of discoloured or damp plasterwork, rotten timbers or window frames.

- Extensive cracking in solid walls or plasterwork. Hairline cracks are inevitable, but if cracks are wider and particularly if they continue to widen there may be an underlying structural fault.
- Fine bore holes in woodwork or furniture.
- Frequent short-circuits or blown fuses.

COSMETIC IMPROVEMENT

Most home improvements fall into this category, for the simple reason that they are relatively inexpensive, easy to execute and provide more or less instant results. Options include:

- Redecorating walls, ceilings and woodwork.
- Repairing or renewing battered or cracked surfaces, such as replastering walls or refinishing wood floors.
- Recovering upholstered furniture.
- Renewing soft furnishings, such as curtains, blinds and loose covers.
- Replacing floor coverings or laying new floors.
- Adding new drawer fronts to fitted units.
- Improving furniture arrangement.
- Installing better lighting.

Spatial changes to the structure of your home are the most complex, often the most expensive and certainly the most disruptive that you are likely to undertake. Here a new mezzanine level has been created to provide self-contained areas within an open-plan space. A particular feature of the design is the central spiral stair that provides both access to the upper level and a striking focus of interest.

REPLANNING AND REORGANISING

Many problems can be corrected by making better use of existing space. This is an area of improvement that is often overlooked, which is all the more surprising when you consider how dramatic the difference can be. Options include:

■ Redesignating room use. An under-used dining room might make a better study, particularly if your kitchen is large enough to eat in. A bright first-floor bedroom might make a better living area than a darker room downstairs, which may well be adequate for a bedroom.

■ Reviewing your possessions. Force yourself to have a big clear-out from time to time: it's one of the simplest ways to gain more space.

■ Planning better storage. Install built-in cupboards and exploit out-of-the-way locations such as the area under the stairs to keep clutter under control.

■ Replanning routes. Block up doorways that you never use to gain wall space.

If you are feeling the pinch, you may find the extra space you need by converting an attic (LEFT). Roof lights set in the sloping plane of the roof are relatively simple to install. Creating a mezzanine level (RIGHT) is a good way to subdivide a double-height space.

A glazed walkway provides a dramatic connection between an existing house and its extension (LEFT). Major building projects require specialist help from architects, surveyors and contractors.

STRUCTURAL AND SPATIAL CHANGE

The most ambitious and radical alterations fall into this category. But if the rewards are great, there are also plenty of pitfalls. To carry out improvements on this level, you will need nerves of steel, the patience of Job, deep pockets and sound professional advice. It is always essential to get an expert's opinion to determine whether what you are planning is safe, legal and feasible. In the case of major alteration, you may need to seek official consent before you can begin and the work itself may need to be approved by a building inspector. Options include:

■ Changing services, such as creating a new bathroom, moving the kitchen or installing new heating systems.

■ Changing the size or shape of rooms by moving walls, adding partitions or knocking through. The degree of difficulty is determined by whether any of the affected walls are load-bearing or not.

■ Altering the position of a staircase.

■ Changing external openings, such as enlarging or adding new windows.

■ Converting attic or basement areas.

■ Adding on a conservatory, an extension or a new storey.

ACTION
STATIONS

The point of the assessment exercise on page 14 was to identify all potential areas for improvement in a clear and rational way. But emotional factors also come into play. You may feel, for example, that right now redecorating the bathroom is far more important to you than buying a new sofa. At the end of the day, only you can decide where your real priorities lie.

USING A FLOOR PLAN

You won't need an accurate scale drawing of the spare bedroom if all you are intending to do is give it a fresh coat of paint, but in many other instances floor plans are invaluable. A floor plan helps you to juggle furniture arrangement two-dimensionally – which is a lot less backbreaking than doing it the other way. It also gives you a clear starting point for discussions with any professionals you may need to consult.

Instructions for drawing up floor plans and using furniture templates are given on pages 172–73. But here it is worth emphasising the importance of taking accurate measurements – and this applies not only to making plans, but is also relevant when it comes to purchasing large items of furniture or appliances. In purely practical terms, more home improvement disasters can be traced back to wrong measurements than any other cause. If you do not trust your skills in this department, ask a numerate friend to help you. Check, recheck and remember the carpenter's saying: 'measure twice, cut once'. But you do not have to be a dunce at arithmetic to get your figures wrong – just consider those red-faced NASA scientists when the failure of the Mars probe turned out to rest on a basic muddle of metric and imperial. Choose one system of measurement and stick to it.

Careful planning is the best way to avoid home improvement disasters. Make sure you take accurate measurements, check your arithmetic and work out a detailed budget before you commit yourself to a course of action.

DRAWING UP A BUDGET

If you are having certain difficulties deciding which improvements to carry out, money matters may focus your mind considerably. A budget consists of two parts: what you can reasonably afford and what your proposals will cost.

Decide what you can afford to spend first. There are different ways of financing improvements, from using a lump sum (savings, for example), to borrowing the money in the form of some kind of loan. Loans vary from relatively expensive in-store credit to cheaper and more long-term arrangements. If you are prepared to be very disciplined, you may even be able to fund your proposals by reining back expenditure in other areas – foregoing the new car, for example, or the annual holiday.

The other side of the equation is the cost of what you are proposing to do. Whatever the scale of the project, make sure you do your research properly. If it is a simple decorating job and you intend to do the work yourself, work out the cost of materials and the cost of your time. For work on a larger scale, which involves contractors, you must get estimates from at least three different companies.

Go over those estimates with a fine toothcomb. Make sure they include the cost of labour and materials, right down to what may seem insignificant details, such as light switches and handles – you will wind up being charged for them, whatever happens, so it is important to know up front what they are likely to cost. Don't forget to include the cost of borrowing money, if that is how you intend to proceed, any fees from design consultants and an allowance for inconvenience – the cost of eating out while a kitchen is out of commission, for example. Finally, add on a percentage – between five and ten per cent is usual – for 'contingency'.

Many projects proceed smoothly from start to finish, entirely according to plan. Others throw up surprises – your builder may uncover a leaking pipe, the flooring you have specified may be out of stock and the alternative may be more expensive. With a contingency allowance, you're covered.

The moment of truth comes when you compare what you can afford with the total costs of your proposals. Human nature is such that they are bound not to tally – we all have a tendency to think we can get more for our money.

Bringing the two figures in line can be achieved in various ways:

■ Simplify your plans. Even if you do not intend to employ an architect or designer to oversee the work or draw up a complete scheme, it can be worthwhile spending a little money on consultation to see if there is an easier and more economical route to what you want.

■ Stage the work. Establish which improvements are really essential and tackle them first; postpone the rest until you can afford them.

■ Think laterally. Some of the most ingenious and creative solutions have been inspired by working to tight budgets.

■ Don't cut corners. It ends up costing money.

Some improvements are very disruptive. Changes to basic services, such as plumbing or electricity, can put certain key areas of the home, such as kitchens and bathrooms, out of commission for a while. Make sure you have alternative arrangements in place.

Installing new flooring may involve professional help. Don't be tempted to cut costs by specifying substandard materials, or taking on more than you are qualified to do.

DEVISING A SCHEDULE

The consumer society has accustomed us to more or less instant gratification. For many people, waiting is simply no longer an option. Time, however, is built into the experience of home improvement and the best results are rarely achieved overnight.

If you are doing-it-yourself, your time is your own to plan. You can snatch spare moments to paint the bedroom walls or to shop for new kitchen units, spend a holiday weekend wallpapering the dining room or sew cushion covers in the evenings in front of the television. This relatively unstructured freedom, however, must be tempered with common

sense. It is just as important not to rush things as it is not to cut corners financially. Allow enough time for preparation and for all the stages required to complete the work to a proper standard. An equal temptation is to leave a job half-completed, ready to be finished on the next rainy day. If at all possible, set aside time to see the job through.

It is an altogether more complicated matter when you are employing others. Most people dread escalating costs, but an even more common cause for complaint is the overrun schedule. Few things in life are more frustrating than watching helplessly from the sidelines as the days drag by and the job still isn't completed.

Some delays are unavoidable – and the best you can do is grit your teeth and wait it out. Others can be prevented, or at least anticipated, by a little forethought and preparation. A good starting point is to acquaint yourself with what the proper sequence of events should be. Much needless waste of time and money occurs when work is done in the wrong order. It's foolhardy, for example, to arrange for a new carpet to be laid and then decide to decorate the walls. All jobs vary, according to the complexity of the project, but the order of work should follow this sequence:

■ Clearing the area of furniture and ornaments, protecting existing surfaces and finishes, stripping out redundant features or demolishing walls.
■ Making new external connections to services, such as gas, water or electricity.
■ Major internal building work, including building new partitions or structural walls, laying concrete or solid floors.
■ Installing boilers, pipework or new wiring.
■ Preliminary carpentry, including doors and window frames.
■ Plastering.

Redecoration may appear a simple prospect, but the hidden part of the job lies in the preparation required. Poor wall and ceiling surfaces will need to be filled, sanded down and possibly lined with lining paper before you can start painting. Tedious though it may be, time devoted to preparation makes a huge difference to the final effect.

■ Installing bathroom and kitchen fittings. Installing radiators.

■ Hanging new doors and installing woodwork, such as mouldings or skirting boards. Building in cupboards, shelves or fitted units.

■ Sanding floorboards.

■ Preparatory decoration: filling, sanding, lining walls, undercoating.

■ Final decoration of walls, ceilings, woodwork.

■ Laying carpeting and other new floor finishes.

■ Furniture arrangement, hanging curtains and blinds, decorative detail.

HIRING HELP

At some stage in every home improvement scheme, there is bound to come a time when you have to call in the professionals. You may need a carpet-layer, an electrician, or a whole team of builders. Whatever assistance is required, the basic principles remain the same.

■ Shop around. Get recommendations. Take up references, ask to see examples of previous work and check professional accreditations.

■ Prepare as specific a brief as possible, detailing the materials, finishes and standard you expect.

■ Ask for a detailed estimate of cost and time. Get three different estimates so you can compare.

■ Once you have decided to employ a contractor or a firm, draw up a written agreement, with all the details spelled out.

■ Arrange payment in stages, with each sum payable upon completion of a given procedure.

■ Agree on a working relationship: times of arrival and departure, access to facilities, storage of tools and materials, cleaning up.

■ When work gets under way, set aside regular times for inspection, but keep out of the way the rest of the time.

■ Don't revise the scheme as you go along. If you change your mind frequently, or add in extra work, you will wind up with additional costs, a protracted schedule and exasperated contractors.

Like many other partnerships, when things get nasty between contractor and client there is often fault on both sides. If you have done your homework, your contractor should be competent and reliable. But he or she also needs your cooperation if everyone is to be happy with the final result.

DESIGN
TOOL
KIT

Both colour and pattern can be used as accents to enliven the interior. An armchair covered in a large floral print makes a focus of interest (ABOVE). A sofa upholstered in a strong solid shade of blue contrasts effectively with a vibrant red wall in an otherwise neutral space (ABOVE RIGHT)

The last chapter looked at the nuts and bolts of assessment, how to plan a campaign of action to turn your ideas into reality. This section goes back to the basic elements in the home decorator's palette: the raw ingredients of colour, texture, pattern, surfaces and finishes and lighting. Orchestrated as a whole, these form the basis of every decorative scheme.

The way we design and decorate our homes is built on precedent. There is the physical fabric of our houses, which may enshrine traditional methods of construction or conventions of spatial planning. In addition, there are overlaying cultural and historical meanings associated with specific patterns, types of room arrangement or furnishings. Then there are common human responses to different qualities of light, colour and form.

Precedent may give you a framework, for a scheme, but it cannot provide the individual or personal quality that is so important. Although it is perfectly possible to copy a decorative look in the same way as you would follow a recipe, the expression of your own personality will be missing.

This chapter picks up where the Introduction left off and is intended to help you to develop your own tastes and preferences into a coherent decorative scheme. Using your collection of 'favourite things' (see page 9) as a basis of inspiration, you can move on to translate your ideas into concrete choices: paint colours, wallpaper or fabric patterns, flooring materials, position and type of light sources. Creating a sample board will enable you to draw your ideas together and move on to the next step.

Geometric patterns, such as stripes, squares and tartan, have a natural affinity with each other (ABOVE). Textural variety is an important part of a successful decorative scheme (ABOVE LEFT).

COLOUR

Colour is one of the most powerful and most expressive of all the decorative tools. We are highly visual creatures and our most dominant sense is sight. Colour, as a signal or identifier, is one of the ways in which we distinguish between different aspects of the world. But colour also provokes emotional responses: it can arouse or soothe, it can inspire peaceful contemplation or strong aversion. It needs to be handled with care.

Colour brings energy to the interior. Exploit the vibrancy of complementary shades to add vitality to your home (ABOVE). Cushions and other accessories can be used to add colour in small doses (RIGHT); while picking out one wall in a strong shade is less dominating than decorating the entire room (FAR RIGHT).

▶ WALLETS

The power of colour is such that many people fight shy of using it altogether, bleaching out their lives to a muted monotone. Neutral decorative schemes can be rich and characterful, particularly when they employ a variety and depth of textures. More often than not, however, they are simply evidence of a lack of nerve. Think how quickly you would lose your appetite if at every meal you were presented with a plate of bland boiled potatoes and white fish. In a similar way, choosing to live in relentlessly neutral surroundings can cut you off from what is, after all, an elemental pleasure. Colour, decoratively speaking, is the spice of life.

Tapping into colour's raw energy does not mean you have to paint your bedroom walls scarlet, or raid the paintbox for searing primary hues. Strong colour can be just as effective in small doses, while the more subtle shades, used on a large scale, can be every bit as revitalising and uplifting.

One difficulty many people experience with colour is the difficulty of making a choice from the wealth of shades offered by manufacturers today. When faced with a myriad of small coloured squares on a paint chart, it is small wonder that off-white can quickly seem the safest bet. The answer is to learn how to use colour to enrich your home.

UNDERSTANDING COLOUR

Colour is not a property of objects – it does not reside in things – but is a function of how our eyes see light. A red apple looks red because it absorbs all the wavelengths of light except red, which is reflected back to our eyes. Light itself contains all the colours of the spectrum, a fact that is easy to appreciate when we see light fractured by a prism into its constituent rainbow of hues.

White light is a blend of equal parts of the spectrum colours. Although this spectrum is in fact continuous, it is usually represented in the distinct colours of red, orange, yellow, green, blue and violet. Each of these has its own wavelength from the shortest, blue, to the longest, red. We cannot see the whole spectrum of light, which extends at either extreme to infrared and ultraviolet; what we find most comfortable is the middle of the range, which approximates to the colours yellow and green. This is in the daylight; as it gets darker, the range of colours that we see most easily shifts to blue. Such inherent physical sensitivities have a bearing on the way we respond to colour in the home.

In artistic terms, red, yellow and blue are primary colours, since all other colours can be mixed from them. As every schoolchild knows, red and yellow make orange, yellow and blue make green and blue and red make purple. These three colours – orange, green and purple – are known as secondary colours. Further mixing of primaries

All-white schemes enhance the sense of light and space. Here, the use of natural materials such as wicker and terracotta, keep the effect from looking bland and insipid (RIGHT).

Use the colour wheel (LEFT) to create a family of related shades. Choose a complementary pair, mix a little of one colour into the other, add white to lighten or black to darken, and you will soon arrive at a softer palette whose basic compatibility rests on that fundamental electric pairing.

and secondaries results in tertiary shades such as terracotta and turquoise, which have an innate edginess. Adding white to any colour will lighten the tone; adding black will darken it.

Colours that have opposite positions on the colour wheel (left) are said to be contrasting or complementary. Complementary pairs include red and green and blue and orange. In their purest form, such pairings have immense power.

For an illustration of the possibilities in decoration, experiment with artists' colours. Pick one of the complementary pairs, then paint blocks of each colour side by side. Then try out different combinations of scale – for example, a large block of red bordered by a narrow band of green or an expanse of green dotted with red. What looks tiring when both colours are used in equal amounts becomes vitalising when one accents the other.

Colour schemes based on tertiary colours, such as terra-cotta, dusky reds and aubergine, make for rich and exotic combinations (LEFT). Tone is an important consideration. Pale or bleached-out colours (RIGHT) are airy and expansive, ideal for a traditional look.

COLOUR ASSOCIATIONS

Colour is not simply a question of scientific or artistic theory: it is also about meaning and association. Many of the responses we have to different colours come from nature; some are cultural; others are embedded deep in our memories.

Broadly speaking, however, colours divide into 'warm' and 'cool'. Warm colours, such as reds, oranges and golden yellows, are said to be 'advancing', which means they leap out at you and attract your attention, which is why you find such shades widely used in commercial packaging,

road signs or any form of communication which needs to stand out. By contrast, cool colours, such as blues, blue–greens, greys and violets, are 'distancing'. They imply spaciousness and reserve and turn the emotional temperature right down.

You can exploit such basic differences between families of colour in the home. Warm advancing shades make great accent colours on cushions, and throws and as trimming and edging. Cool distant colours enhance the sense of space and provide peaceful backgrounds in situations where there is a good level of natural light.

Red equals ripeness, danger, alert, display, celebration, excitement and energy. In Eastern cultures, it is the colour of ceremony and marriage. In large amounts, red can be tiring and over-stimulating.

Yellow is sunny and uplifting. The citrus shades of lemon, lime and orange are fresh and cheerful; deeper, more golden colours have an inbuilt richness. Yellow is a difficult colour to get right and you may need to experiment to find the shade that best suits your lighting conditions.

Green is one of nature's most common colours and is the shade our eyes find most comfortable. For this reason, it has a certain restful quality, particularly the darker shades. Leaf green can be very fresh, especially used with plenty of white. As a background colour green can be dispiriting and rather bilious looking, particularly in the kitchen.

Blue is airy and expansive, the colour of the sea, the distant horizon and the sky. Use wherever there is good natural light to make a room seem bigger. In dark rooms, however, blues can be chilly and depressing. Traditionally, dairies and kitchens featured plenty of blue since the colour was thought to act as a fly repellent.

■ Earth tones are inherently associated with natural materials, from rich terracottas to dark woody shades of teak and oak. Depending on texture and style, they can be rustic and countrified, or svelte and sophisticated.

■ Neutrals, from the many shades of grey and off-white to pure white and black act as mediators in a decorative scheme. White has a freshening effect: think of red and white checked tablecloths or blue and white crockery. Black, especially in the form of trimming or edging, adds graphic definition, particularly in rooms with Eastern overtones.

CREATING A COLOUR SCHEME

Most of us know what colours we like; it's when we think about putting together a colour scheme that we tend to come unstuck. Liking a colour isn't the same as living with it day after day. Whether or not it will be successful in the context of your home depends on a variety of factors, not least of which are the existing lighting conditions.

First, go back to your collection to see if there is a common denominator in terms of colour or mood. A prevalence of seascape images might suggest a marine palette of misty blues, blue–greys and

A variety of neutral, natural tones (LEFT) make for a harmonious and restful ensemble.

Yellow is sunny and uplifting, particularly in rooms which receive plenty of natural light. Here (RIGHT), the mellow tones of wooden furniture and flooring complement the basic decorative scheme.

blue–greens, partnered with white or neutral sandy shades. On the other hand, if you have collected strong graphic shapes in bright colours, you might think about a basic neutral scheme, accented with bold primaries.

Consider the aspect of the room you intend to decorate. How much natural light does it receive and when? Rooms that face north (or south in the southern hemisphere) will need warming up; south-facing rooms can either be decorated in cooler colours if you like a fresh look, or you can use warm tones of yellow to enhance the sunny aspect.

Think about artificial lighting, too. Tungsten light-bulbs have a yellowish cast, which will affect the way you perceive colours after dark. Halogen light sources are whiter in appearance: colour rendering will be truer to nature. When you are collecting samples or painting test patches, remember to view them under conditions of both natural and artificial light – there can often be a surprising difference.

Similarly, colour can help to adjust scale and proportion. Light, cool colours make rooms seem bigger; dark, warm colours provide a sense of enclosure. Although this might seem to indicate that you should decorate a small room in light colours, sometimes the opposite approach can be very effective: a deep, warm background in a small space can be both rich and intimate.

Objects and accessories contribute just as much colour interest as main surfaces and finishes, as demonstrated by this multicolored collection of crockery and table linen.

Although we tend to think of colour almost exclusively in terms of paint, almost every aspect of a room can contribute to a colour scheme: not merely upholstery, curtains and carpets, but also woodwork, built-in features such as kitchen worktops, decorative objects, paintings and flowers. You can paint all your walls white and still be surrounded with colour, if you exploit all the opportunities such elements have to offer.

BASIC STRATEGIES

▦ Use complementary pairs to create a palette of related shades that will provide unity to your decorative scheme. The palest colours can be reserved for backgrounds; the most vivid used for accents.

▦ Increase the sense of space by repeating colours from room to room, so that the blue of the bathroom tiling, for example, crops up in the kitchen in the form of the paintwork on the cupboards. Using colour as a theme throughout your home provides a subtle thread to tie it all together.

▦ Do not rely too heavily on colour coordination. Rooms that are entirely decorated in the same shade can be very exhausting and oppressive places – it is important to provide neutral breathing space.

▦ Play safe when it comes to choosing the colour of large pieces of upholstered furniture, carpeting or any other element which either dominates a room or represents a significant investment. Repainting a wall when you don't like the colour is cheap and straightforward; replacing the flooring is not.

▦ Have fun with accents. Renewable colour, such as fresh flowers and houseplants, throws, or even cushion covers, can help to ring the changes and prevent a static look. What goes on in the foreground often attracts the most attention.

Focal points such as paintings and rugs can provide a starting point for a decorative scheme. Here the colours of soft furnishings and decoration repeat those displayed in the picture on the wall, creating a subtle and unified effect.

PATTERN
AND TEXTURE

All decorative elements are interrelated, but pattern and texture are closer than most. Like colour, they add vitality to the interior, together with an inherent sense of rhythm and movement. At their most forthright, pattern and texture can be as dramatic as the most vivid splash of colour, but in more muted form they can also offer a subconscious sense of security and comfort.

▶ WALLETS

The urge to create patterns is as old as the first handprints daubed on the walls of prehistoric caves. There is something ultimately satisfying about making repetitive marks. At the same time, patterns enshrine a sense of orderliness and arrangement in the very regularity of their designs.

While patterns provide visual texture, different combinations of surfaces and finishes offer a less obvious, but no less important depth of character. Physical texture, revealed in the way light is absorbed or reflected from a surface, or the way it feels to the touch, is a key element in decoration, but one that is often overlooked. This type of textural variety is particularly important where decorative schemes are essentially neutral.

Different textures provide visual variety, revealed in light and shade (RIGHT). But they also contribute enormously to our tactile pleasure. How things feel can be just as important as how they look. A new look for an old favourite – chintz coverings look fresh in a contemporary room (FAR RIGHT).

TYPES OF PATTERN

Soft furnishings offer the greatest opportunity to introduce pattern to the home. The innate liveliness of a repeating design is particularly effective in situations where materials are draped or hung in soft folds. But pattern does not just equal fabric or textiles; other sources include wallpaper, tiling, flooring designs and decorative detail.

Throughout history, people have created a wealth of different patterns. Advances in technology and printing processes mean that we have the opportunity to choose from a wider range of patterns today than ever before; however, the trend for contemporary interiors to be decorated with blocks of solid colour and plain materials means that the use of pattern is not as prevalent as it was.

Many patterns have a specific cultural or historic reference point, which demands an appropriate setting. The dense, naturalistic designs of William Morris are indelibly late Victorian; delicate Chinoiserie-style patterns of flowers and birds have a brittle eighteenth-century elegance. Sprigged patterns of rosebuds or nosegays have a cottagey appeal. Few of these work out of context.

Geometric designs, however, are more adaptable. Stripes were a feature of Regency decor but work equally well in a contemporary setting where they can suggest everything from refinement to a more jaunty, irreverent quality. Star patterns can similarly be elegant and rather grand, or more reminiscent of a Moorish influence. Checked patterns, from the homely, domestic gingham to traditional tartans and madras, are among the most versatile – and ancient in origin – of all.

Primitive patterns, such as the abstracted designs typically seen in native rugs or wallhangings, introduce a bold, earthy quality to the interior. Many such designs are equally at home in contemporary or more traditionally decorated rooms. Animal-skin prints, such as leopard skin or zebra skin have a similar aesthetic.

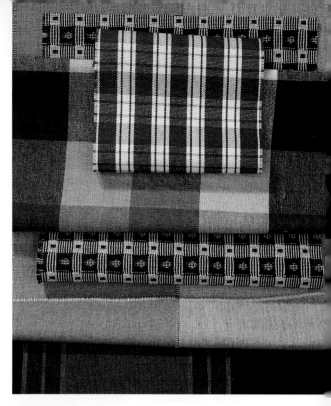

Geometric patterns vary in scale and complexity (ABOVE), but work well together. Combine with plain surfaces and fabrics to provide a little visual breathing space. Figurative or organic patterns (LEFT) are immensely appealing. Combine patterns which share similar colours or have similar themes.

Few of us have the courage to combine colour and pattern with quite the verve demonstrated in this sun-filled room (RIGHT).

USING PATTERN

As with colour, the art of using pattern lies in making sympathetic combinations. Consider the type of each print, its colours and the scale of the design.

▪ The simplest way to use pattern is as an accent. This is often the best strategy in ultra-modern surroundings, where the emphasis is generally on plain surfaces and solid colour. One feature rug or wallhanging can serve as a dramatic focal point.

▪ To create a unified soft-furnishing scheme, select one pattern for a principal decorative element – such as a window treatment – and combine it with a selection of plain or textured fabrics that repeat the colours in your chosen design.

▪ For a more ambitious scheme, think about combining different types of design. Simple geometric prints work well with figurative patterns, provided they share the same colours.

▪ Vary the scale of the patterns you use. Large-scale designs are dominating and can be tiring if used extensively.

▪ You can also combine patterns that share a basic affinity of theme, such as a selection of floral prints of different scales but similar colours. Oriental textiles can be layered for an exotic look.

TEXTURAL VARIETY

Combinations of different textures provide depth
and character in a way that might not be immediately obvious. Texture operates almost on a subconscious level and connects us through senses other
than sight to the natural world.

Uniformity of texture can be deadening or brutal-
ising. A room exclusively upholstered and carpeted
in soft materials might seem in time a little like a
padded cell; while one where the surfaces and
finishes were relentlessly hard would quickly put
your teeth on edge. Textural variety really comes
into its own, however, where the decorative
scheme is pared down and minimal. Neutral
schemes run the real risk of becoming bland
without a forthright display of different types of
surface and finish.

The best source of texture comes in the form of
natural materials, which not only have inbuilt character, but also have the potential to age with charm
and grace. A well-loved and well-scrubbed oak
table, for example, simply gets better with time.
Synthetic materials, on the other hand, generally do
not weather at all attractively.

USING TEXTURE

■ Pay attention to those elements that you touch.
Natural fibres, such as cotton, linen and silk offer
unbeatable comfort next to the skin. Avoid an over-
reliance on synthetic materials, which can have a
lifeless quality.

■ Use texture to make a contrast. A rugged stone
hearth will stand out against smooth plastered
walls; metal or glass splashbacks combine well

Soft furnishings, such as upholstery, throws, curtains and cushion covers, are an important source of texture in the home and create a sense of comfort and security (ABOVE LEFT).

with wooden countertops. Cushions covered in different materials can help to ring the changes.

In a sequence of small spaces, it is often important to keep the floor the same basic colour throughout to provide a unifying factor. However, the flooring materials do not have to be the same: you can combine, for example, pale natural fibre flooring with light wood and cream ceramic tiles for a visually seamless but characterful look that relies on textural variety for impact.

Texture really comes into its own when the basic colour scheme is muted or natural (ABOVE). Different textures reflect light in different ways, an inherent variety that prevents monochromatic schemes from appearing bland or boring.

SURFACES
AND FINISHES

After considering the basic elements of colour, pattern and texture in isolation, it is time to translate some of these preferences into real material choices. Different materials do different jobs, both practically and aesthetically; many can be used in unexpected ways for extra decorative flair.

The use of timber panelling accentuates the planes of walls and ceiling. The effect of the narrow boards is to create a certain subtle rhythm and a feeling of cosiness.

▶ WALLETS   ▶ NOTEBOOK

PRACTICAL CONSIDERATIONS

Materials vary in the degree of punishment they can take, which may rule out certain choices. Think about the amount of wear they are likely to receive, ease of maintenance and safety factors.

WALLS AND CEILINGS

■ In kitchens and bathrooms wall surfaces should be as waterproof as possible. Solutions include: water-resistant or oil-based paint; tile, glass, perspex or metal splashbacks; full-scale or part tiling, or panellinging in tongue-and-groove.

■ Choose a washable finish for children's rooms to enable you to clean off scribbles or fingerprints.

■ Hallways often take a beating. It can be a good idea to protect the lower part of the wall with a dado of wood panelling or a robust wallpaper.

FLOORS

■ Choose non-slip flooring in areas that are likely to become wet, particularly kitchens, bathrooms and entrances. Avoid the use of soft materials, such as carpet or natural fibre flooring, as they are likely to become stained and may rot.

Mosaic tiles laid in a random fashion contribute colour and pattern (LEFT).

The understated elegance of this contemporary living room (RIGHT) owes a great deal to a successful combination of materials and the restrained style of soft furnishing and window treatment.

■ Avoid the use of certain densely piled or textured materials on the stairs where they may cause people to catch their heels and trip. Deep or shaggy pile carpet, boucle natural weaves and thick coir matting are all unsuitable for stair use.

■ Heavy flooring materials, such as stone, may require solid sub-floors. If you plan to use stone on an upper level, where the subfloor is likely to be timber, check with a surveyor first.

■ If you use hard flooring on upper levels, you may create a noise problem in downstairs areas. You may need to add in a sound-insulating layer or opt for a softer, more cushioned solution.

WINDOWS

■ If you find it difficult to sleep unless there is total darkness, opt for blackout blinds or lined curtains.

■ Where the maximum light is required, but privacy is an issue, screen windows with adjustable Venetian or slatted wooden blinds, lightweight semi-transparent curtains or replace standard window glass with frosted or etched glass.

■ Recessed windows can be difficult to curtain. Hinged rods that swing clear of the frame are one solution. Roman or roller blinds are also practical.

■ Toughened glass is a good choice for windows at ground level where there is risk of break-ins.

MATERIAL CHOICES

Thorough research pays off when it comes to selecting materials. Within each broad category of material, there are many different types of product, which may vary widely in specification, price and ease of supply. Conventional outlets include decorating superstores and DIY shops, department and home furnishing stores and retailers specialising in a single type of material, such as carpeting or glass. Less conventional sources include architectural salvage yards for reclaimed timber, stone and tile, secondhand shops for antique textiles and markets for cheap materials and fabrics. Use the Notebook to note the names and numbers of suppliers and to compare prices.

Crisp white woodwork makes the perfect foil for walls painted in a warm shade of yellow. The dado rail, set at a level approximately one-third of the wall height up from the floor, is the traditional means of protecting the wall from the scraping of chair backs.

PAINT

Paint provides an instant cover-up for almost every kind of surface. Modern manufacturers offer every conceivable colour, but you can also have shades mixed to order, or mix colours yourself. Paint is also available in different finishes, from matt to mid-sheen to gloss and in either oil- or water-based formulations. Oil-based paint is harder wearing and is the traditional choice for interior woodwork. Water-based paint is easier to apply and faster drying. Fresh plasterwork or exposed wood should be primed first with a suitable undercoat to seal the surface and prevent excess absorption of paint.

Specialist paints are available to suit a wide variety of different surfaces, from tile and ceramic to metal and glass. There are also a number of

Colourwashed plaster makes an appealingly rustic surface reminiscent of fresco (LEFT). Raw plaster can be sealed with wax for a luminous effect. Brightly painted chairs make a vivid accent in an otherwise neutral scheme (RIGHT).

small suppliers who market special decorative paints, from those that dry to a 'suede' or sandy finish to those that have the chalky appearance of traditional limewash or distemper. Natural paints, made from biodegradable ingredients and containing no chemicals, are available from suppliers of environmentally friendly materials.

PAPER

Many designs of wallpaper are marketed with matching decorative borders and friezes for a complete look. For humid locations, choose a coated paper with a wipable surface. Textured papers have a retro appeal and can work well as dados, particularly in areas of the home which are subject to wear, such as hallways.

There is a huge variety of patterns on the market, with the emphasis mainly on traditional designs, although contemporary prints are also increasingly available. Whichever style appeals, remember that large repeating designs are best used in larger rooms, or the effect can be overwhelming. For a more lateral approach, you can also paper walls with brown paper, Japanese grass papers, foil papers, even maps, posters or art papers – anything that is robust enough to be glued without disintegrating.

Even if you intend to paint your walls, it is often a good idea to line them first with plain lining paper for a smooth surface. Very poor plasterwork can be disguised by cross-lining, which consists of papering in both horizontal and vertical directions.

Wood-panelled walls and ceiling create a sense of enclosure for a sleeping corner, accessorised with vivid check blankets and cushions.

Hardwood floors (RIGHT) are exceptionally elegant, durable and long lasting, advantages that more than offset their considerable price-tag.

FABRIC

Choose the right weight of material for the job it has to perform: upholstering sofas will demand the hardest wearing fabrics, for example.

Many furnishing departments carry a wide range of different types of fabric, from sheer butter muslins to robust linen union and furnishing velvet. But it is also worth experimenting with more unusual materials. Canvas and striped cotton duck make crisp blinds with a nautical appeal; saris and embroidered dress materials can be used to create theatrical window drapery; antique shawls and patchwork quilts can be used as throws.

Fabric lends itself to trimming with contrast banding, braid, fringes and tassels. Such passementerie provides an elegant finishing touch for formal curtains or traditional styles of upholstery.

WOOD

Wood is an exceptionally versatile material and an exceptionally varied one. Often used as a structural element, it is also the basis of many fitted pieces, such as kitchen units, shelving and other integral features. As a decorative surface, wood can be used as flooring, cladding or panelling and in the form of counters, worktops, screens or shutters.

Many different species are suitable for use in the home. The basic distinction is between hardwoods and softwoods. Softwoods, such as pine, are less hard-wearing and are often used in basic construction. Hardwoods are more expensive but often exceptionally attractive. It is important, however, to choose hardwoods that come from sustainably managed plantations; many species are now endangered. As well as solid timber, there are a number of manufactured woods, from laminate to medium-density fibreboard (MDF), a dimensionally stable product that makes excellent shelving, cupboard doors and built-in features.

WOOD FLOORING OPTIONS INCLUDE:

▨ Existing wooden floorboards, sanded and sealed with wax or varnish, stained or painted.

▨ New wood strip floors in solid timber. Species include oak, maple, cherry, beech and birch. Planks are available in different thicknesses, widths and methods of laying.

▨ Parquet or wood block floors, new or reclaimed.

▨ Laminated wood floors, which consist of a thin veneer of wood glued to a layered base. These formats are relatively inexpensive, highly wear-resistant and easy to install, if a little synthetic looking.

▨ Marine plywood can be used as a final floor.

STONE

Stone is a sublime natural material that conveys a sense of permanence to the interior. It is, however, cold, hard to work, expensive, heavy and utterly lacking in resilience. The most common application is again for flooring; you will almost certainly need a specialist to lay a stone floor and you may need to consult a surveyor to establish whether the subfloor can bear the weight. Different types of stone also make elegant and hard-wearing counter-tops for kitchens and bathrooms.

Types of flooring stone include limestone, sand-stone, granite and slate. Formats range from slabs to tiles, which are thinner, cheaper and lighter.

TILE AND BRICK

Brick can make a good-looking and practical floor, particularly in hallways and garden rooms. Terracotta tiles, including quarried and traditional handmade varieties, share a similar aesthetic.

Ceramic tiles have a crisp, contemporary appearance. Tiles for flooring use should be as non-slip as possible; by contrast, wall tiles are generally smooth and highly glazed. Other appli-cations include worktops, splashbacks and areas of part tiling around sinks and bathtubs.

The size of the tile has a bearing on the way the finished result will look. Choose small tiles for a restricted area; larger tiles suit larger expanses.

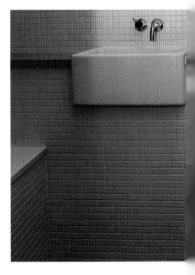

METAL

Metal is a material much associated with sleek, modern interiors. At the simplest, you can use easily worked metals such as zinc as a cladding for kitchen worktops or cupboard doors. Narrow sheets of stainless steel make efficient splashbacks – or you can go the whole hog and opt for fitted stainless steel units, the ultimate in contemporary sophistication (and with a correspondingly high price tag).

Metal, particularly aluminum treadplate, has found a recent use as a flooring material in avant-garde interiors. Though incredibly long-lasting, it is a little brutal for many tastes.

GLASS

One of the most delightful of all materials, glass has a surprisingly wide range of applications in the home: obviously for glazing windows and doors, but also for shelving, as protective wall cladding around sinks and basins, and for pure decorative effect. Glass bricks and blocks can be used structurally to make interior partitions that spill light through from area to area. Toughened, wired or safety glass is a good choice where security is an issue, or where there is a risk of an expanse of glass shattering – in French windows, for example. Stained, etched, coloured and frosted glass adds decorative uplift to windows and fanlights.

In contemporary design, materials take centre stage. A dramatic use of slate to create an integral sink, draining board and splashback, adds graphic punch (FAR LEFT). A regular grid of small ceramic tiles makes a practical bathroom surface (LEFT). Glass bricks have an industrial edge (RIGHT). They serve to admit light while retaining an element of privacy.

SHEET MATERIALS AND SOFT TILES

Chiefly used for flooring, many of these materials are affordable, practical and easy to maintain, which makes them popular decorative choices.

 Linoleum is available in a wide range of colours and patterns and has the bonus of being an entirely natural product. Hygienic, long-lasting and good for kitchen and bathroom floors and worksurfaces, it is available in sheet or tile form.

 Vinyl is lino's synthetic cousin. Designs simulate natural materials, but bright colours and geometric patterns are also available. Vinyl comes in sheet or tile, is generally cheap and often wears poorly.

 Rubber makes a hard-wearing floor with a high-tech industrial look. Many types have relief patterns; a range of solid colours is available.

 Cork makes a warm, resilient floor for kitchens and bathrooms and can also be used as a decorative and practical wall cladding.

The floor is one of the most defining elements in the interior. Studded rubber, with its overtones of high-tech, is a hard-wearing and practical choice for working areas (RIGHT). Floor lights set into the skirting boards accentuate the sinuous path of this carpeted hallway (CENTRE RIGHT). A natural fibre mat makes an effective contrast to a wooden floor (FAR RIGHT).

CARPET

Soft flooring, such as carpet or natural fibre coverings, adds an extra layer of comfort to the home. Carpeting varies widely in quality and hence expense, from all-wool versions to wool/synthetic blends that are often harder wearing. Different weights of carpet are recommended for different areas in the home: choose the hardest wearing for stairs and halls or wherever traffic is heaviest; bedroom carpets can be lighter and softer. Carpet comes in scores of different colours, patterns and textures to suit every taste, from velvety cut pile to looped variegated Berber.

Natural fibre coverings have provided an alternative to carpeting ever since they became available in a wall-to-wall format. Types of fibre range from coarse coir to silky smooth jute. Sisal, which can be dyed and comes in a range of patterns and weaves, is among the most popular. These materials often stain and can be rather expensive.

LIGHTING

One of the most radical alterations you can make to your home is to change the way it is lit. Lighting has a profound effect on our sense of comfort and well-being, an effect that operates almost subconsciously; equally important, the way you light different spaces within your home has a great impact on how easy or otherwise it is to perform certain essential tasks.

If many people are unaware of lighting's decorative potential and its key role in generating mood and atmosphere, there is also a common tendency to focus on the style or design of the light fitting itself, regardless of the type of light it emits. It is far from uncommon for light fittings to be purchased without once being switched on.

Lighting design has made great strides in recent decades and a greater choice, both of fittings and light sources, is now available for use in the home. If you find lighting technology a little off-putting, take the time to visit a lighting showroom and ask for a demonstration before making a final selection.

Light animates the interior. The most successful lighting schemes are those that provide something of the same variety of conditions one would expect to experience outdoors. Different light levels and directions generate vitality and promote atmosphere.

CREATING A LIGHTING SCHEME

Most people tend to equate a poorly lit space with one where there is an insufficient level of lighting. But it can also be one where the lighting is too bright or too glaring, or one where lights are in the wrong places and performing the wrong functions. If anything, most homes today are overlit and yet have too few sources of light. Before you get down to selecting light fittings or even deliberating about the types of light sources you require, it is important to consider the space as a whole from the point of view of both function and aesthetics. Use the graph paper to help you to plot out lighting arrangements for different rooms in conjunction with furniture layouts and built-in features, referring to the instructions given on pages 172–73.

Tea lights set in old jam jars make charming, improvised garden lanterns. Soft and mobile, candlelight turns an event into an occasion.

DESIGN GUIDELINES

■ Increase the number of light sources. A single very bright light may supply the same level of illumination as four or five dimmer lights, but the effect will be static and unpleasant.

■ Create pools of light and shade. Positioning lights around the room and at different levels, draws the eye from place to place, creating glowing focal points and accentuating textures.

■ Avoid glare. Glare is tiring on the eyes and psychologically disturbing. Use directional fittings to bounce light off expanses of walls and ceilings for a soft background illumination. Choose pendant or overhead fittings very carefully so that the light source is not directly visible. You can also hide light sources completely behind baffles.

■ Establish where more concentrated lighting is required. Specific tasks, such as preparing food and specific areas, such as the desktop, chairside or bedside, often require directional light that can be targeted at the worksurface or task in hand.

■ Plan for flexibility. Lighting track, where individual lights can be repositioned as need dictates, often provides greater long-term adaptability than fixed arrangements, such as downlighters. Fitting dimmer switches multiplies the effects you can create and enables you to adjust lighting levels according to mood or time of day.

■ Don't neglect the impact of natural sources of lighting. The flickering flames of a real fire, or soft candlelight, provides unbeatable atmosphere.

Recessed downlights are among the most inobtrusive of fittings (FAR LEFT). Slatted blinds allow you to adjust the levels of natural light. Standard or table lamps offer local light where it is needed, as well as a focus of interest.

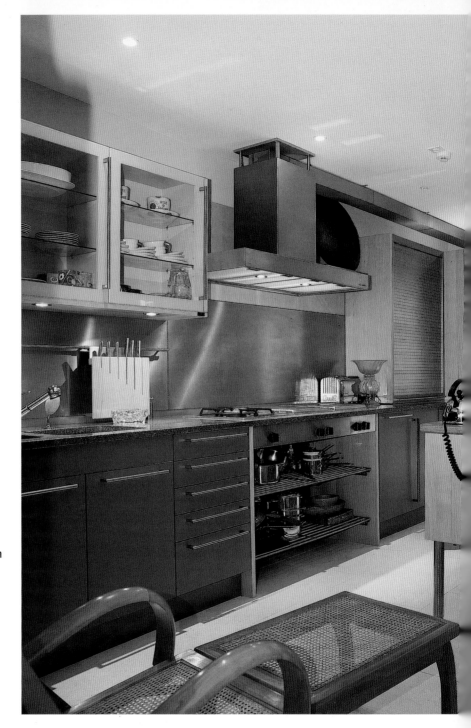

Hard-working areas of the home, such as kitchens, demand careful planning when it comes to lighting. You will need bright, shadow-free task lighting over work surfaces, together with a good general level of background illumination. Downlights recessed in the ceiling and under wall-hung kitchen units deliver light where it is required.

TYPES OF LIGHTING

Broadly speaking, lights can be classified into different types according to the functions they perform. Most areas in the home will need a combination of several or all of these types, both to work effectively and to look good.

▧ Background or ambient lighting is simply the type of lighting that makes it possible to see when night falls. It can be achieved in various ways: by reflecting light off walls and ceilings, by means of pendants or wall-mounted fittings that emit an omni-directional glow, or by positioning a series of directional lights which together serve to increase the overall level of illumination. Background lighting on its own can be bland and featureless.

▧ Task lighting is work-related and often directional. The classic example is the angled desk lamp, which can be positioned to shine where it is required; similarly, downlights positioned over a countertop constitute task lighting. The crucial factor is to make sure the light source is concealed to avoid hurting your eyes and to position the light so that you are not working in your own shadow. Because of their directional nature, task lights create strong contrasts of light and dark, that can be uncomfortable without supplementary sources.

▧ Accent lighting performs a decorative role, enhancing architectural features or decorative displays. But decorative lights – lights that essentially light up only themselves – can also be a form of accent lighting in their own right, adding a sculptural sense to the interior.

▧ Information lighting adds to the safety and practicality of the home. Most of these types of lights perform a specific function – from the light in the refrigerator to the light over the front door.

CHOOSING LIGHT SOURCES

In technical terms, the light source is what makes the light: it is the artificial equivalent of the sun. Until fairly recently, the only light source available for domestic use was the familiar tungsten-filament bulb or GLS (general lighting service) lamp. Today, new lighting sources provide different colours and qualities of light, different degrees of energy efficiency and different lifespans.

TUNGSTEN bulbs are cheap, widely available, easy to use and produce a warm, yellowish light. They come in a range of sizes, shapes and wattages, light up instantly and require no additional control gear. On the downside, they convert most of their energy into heat, which means that they cannot be used close to flammable materials, such as paper or fabric. They are the most short-lived and least energy-efficient of all light sources.

TUNGSTEN HALOGEN (usually known as 'halogen') is a light source that was originally used in retail environments. It emits a sparkling white light that represents colours more faithfully than tungsten. There are two principal varieties: mains-voltage and low-voltage. Mains-voltage halogen can be run directly off the mains, but is less widely available and tends to generate a lot of heat. Low-voltage halogen requires a transformer to step the power down, but bulbs are smaller and more compact and consequently work well for accent or display lighting. These bulbs are cheaper to run and more energy efficient than tungsten.

Practically speaking **FLUORESCENTS** have always scored highly, being economical, long-lasting and energy-efficient. The problem was that they looked so terrible. The main reason is that standard fluorescent light is skewed so that overall it has a greenish cast, which gives it both poor colour rendering and a brutal, unappealing appearance. The lights also had a tendency to flicker and hum. New designs increasingly address these aesthetic disadvantages and provide a better quality of light. They are also available in formats that allow them to be used as a substitute for tungsten in ordinary fittings. For the ecologically conscious, the great advantage of the new compact or mini-fluorescents is their exceptionally low energy use, which also means that they cost little to operate.

CHOOSING LIGHT FITTINGS

The light fitting – in technical terms, known as the 'luminaire' – fulfils two basic functions. First and foremost, it directs and controls the spread of light from the light source itself. Secondly, and most obviously, it provides a vehicle for style.

Light fittings come in every conceivable fashion, from antique crystal chandeliers to matt black high-tech task lights; from unobtrusive recessed halogen spots to sculptural floor lights that provide a focal point in themselves. But while style is an important issue, familiarising yourself with the types of fitting available will help ensure you choose the right light for the job it has to do.

Artificial light should complement natural light from windows and skylights. Here wall-mounted uplights enhance the effect of light spilling through the glazed roof and gable end.

UPLIGHTS

DOWNLIGHTS

WALL LIGHTS

CENTRAL LIGHTS

UPLIGHTS or uplighters direct most or all of their light upwards, where it is reflected from the ceiling to create a soft, ambient glow. The effect is to accentuate the sense of volume in a space. Uplighting can also be used to emphasise textural contrast, and is particularly good at providing glare-free light where computer screens are in use. Any directional light angled upwards makes an uplighter. Other types include floor-standing uplights, drum uplights, and wall-mounted uplights.

DOWNLIGHTS or downlighters generally comprise a range of fittings that direct a tight beam of light downwards to illuminate a specific area. They are best used in areas such as kitchens where features are built in and flexibility is not an issue. Fittings may be recessed or mounted on the surface; some are fixed and others are adjustable.

WALL LIGHTS make use of the plane of the wall to reflect light and create background illumination. There is a wide range of styles available, from traditional shaded sconces, to wall-mounted uplights of various designs. Most wall lights emit light in more than one direction and look good in pairs or in symmetrical arrangements.

CENTRAL LIGHTS create a focus for a room, but must be used in conjunction with other sources of light to avoid creating a flat, deadened look. In the case of pendant fittings, make sure that the fitting conceals the bulb from direct view or there will be a risk of glare. Rise and fall pendants are available that allow the height of the light to be adjusted.

FLOOR LAMPS or standard lamps introduce a height variable to your lighting scheme, which can help to break up relentless horizontal lines. The standard lamp, which formerly had a rather old-fashioned image, has recently been revived in a number of classic modern designs.

TABLE LAMPS range from decorative objects that just happen to supply light, to hard-working task lights that deliver precise illumination to working areas. In traditional designs, the focus of interest is generally the lamp base, which may be in the shape of a candlestick, urn, vase, column or sculpture.

SPOTLIGHTS provide an indispensable accent to a lighting scheme. Spots can be recessed, surface mounted, used singly, in pairs or in multiples. Many are adjustable, allowing light to be directed.

FLOOR LAMPS

SPOTLIGHTS

TABLE LAMPS

Different light fittings emit light in different ways, a factor that is more relevant when it comes to creating a lighting scheme than the actual style and appearance of the design.

PUTTING A SAMPLE BOARD TOGETHER

The sample board is a presentational tool used by professional designers and decorators. Its essential purpose is to serve as an accessible way of showing preliminary ideas to a client, ready for subsequent discussion. But you do not have to be a professional to benefit from the same process. The sample board is simply a more concrete version of your cuttings file, the means by which you translate tastes and preferences into real choices.

To put a sample board together, you will need to collect swatches of fabric, samples of materials such as tiles or other types of flooring, sample pots of paint and decorative trimmings. Assemble them on a piece of stiff cardboard to assess how well they work together. It helps if you display them in the scale in which you intend to use them: for example, if you are uphol-stering a sofa in one print and using another design for cushion covers, the first swatch should be much larger than the second to give you some idea how the proportions will work together.

Once you have assembled your sample board, place it in a prominent position. Materials and colours look different under different lighting condi-tions, so you will need a certain amount of time to make a proper consideration.

ROOM
BY ROOM
STYLE

The time has come to apply the basic principles outlined in the previous chapters and translate your overall strategy into specific courses of action. This section takes you through each area in the home, pinpointing essential practicalities and potential decorative solutions.

Most of us still live in homes conventionally subdivided into rooms designated for particular functions. The reasons are pretty clear. Our familiar domestic blueprint, fine-tuned over centuries, continues to serve us well and provides a welcome sense of continuity and reassurance.

At the same time, there is no getting away from the fact that there has been a certain blurring of boundaries in recent years as lifestyles have changed. The decline of formal dining has seen a corresponding decline in the dining room as a separate entity, with eating areas increasingly absorbed into living spaces or kitchens. The trend for working at home has added another factor into the equation; where space is too tight to convert a room into a home office, work areas have crept into bedrooms, living rooms, and even kitchens. The fashion for multi-purpose open-plan arrangement, which originated in the immediate postwar period, has recently been boosted by the popularity of 'loft-style' living where spaces flow into one another without the defining element of walls.

Whatever your decorative tastes, your home must accommodate a range of basic activities from eating to bathing and relaxing. In the past, homes featured a number of self-contained rooms, each assigned a different function. Today, the trend is for multi-purpose spaces that provide room for several activities.

But however your home is arranged, you can't get away from the fact that you will inevitably require specific areas for cooking, eating, bathing, sleeping, relaxing – the fundamental human activities for which all homes must cater. If you begin by looking at the functions each space must fulfil, the final result will have much more clarity. These practicalities will also have an impact on decorative decisions – a living room that must accommodate a large family is bound to look different from one where the only person to please is yourself.

The other point to bear in mind as you begin to come up with a scheme for each area is the time factor. It is worth trying to imagine how your life might change in the future so that you can build in a degree of flexibility. In this sense, a home can fit too perfectly, ruling out any adjustments a change in lifestyle might demand. The best design schemes are always a little open-ended.

The same applies to decoration. The link between fashion and home decoration is continually stressed these days, and there is no doubt that both spheres have grown ever closer. But while it is relatively painless to accept that last season's wardrobe looks a little dated when the new styles come out, most people expect more longevity and better value from their decorative choices at home.

List problem areas in your Notebook, and use it to record suppliers and keep track of progress.

As you proceed from area to area, use the Graph Paper to sketch plans of each room, noting existing features such as fireplaces, power points and fitted elements (see pages 172–73).

Make scale cut-outs of furniture you wish to buy or retain and experiment with different layouts using the Templates (see pages 174–77).

LIVING ROOMS

Living rooms can suffer from a certain problem of definition, a vagueness with respect to purpose that tends to come across in decoration and design. Where there is lack of clarity, the living room often becomes a muddled catch-all for the activities that cannot be accommodated elsewhere in the home, everything from quiet study to noisy play. The result can end up being a place in which no one truly feels at ease and where competing demands rule out any possibility of harmony, visual or otherwise.

If nothing else, the living room should provide a haven of tranquillity in which to unwind at the end of a long day. A pure white colour scheme (ABOVE) is especially calming.

Comfortably worn leather club chairs and an upholstered armchair (RIGHT) make a companionable grouping.

At the same time, the living room inevitably bears the burden of an enormous raft of expectations. The showcase of our tastes and preferences, the living room serves as the public face of our home, where we are determined to put our best foot forward, decoratively speaking, and where we are prepared to spend more time and money getting it right. Deficiencies we might well tolerate behind the scenes strike a particularly jarring note when they are there for everyone to see. While such concerns are perfectly understandable, if this public role comes to assume too much importance, the living room can become a rather dead and static place, displaying a 'hands off' quality that inevitably means most of the 'living' actually takes place in other areas.

What are living rooms really for? In today's hectic world, we increasingly need our homes to serve as places of refuge and retreat, where we can recharge our batteries, unwind and be ourselves. At the very least, the living room should provide the right conditions for such mental and physical relaxation. And if you feel comfortable, there is a strong possibility that others visiting your home will feel the same way, which, after all, is the best welcome you can provide.

ASSESSING YOUR NEEDS

In your Notebook, make a note of your answers to the following questions. They will help you to assess how many different activities are likely to take place in your living room. If you come up with a number of answers that indicate fundamental incompatibilities, consider using other areas in the home to take up some of the slack. Could you create a study corner in a bedroom, for example? Could you better incorporate a dining area into the kitchen?

If your living room simply must function as a multi-purpose space – however varied those activities might be – you can still prioritise the most important uses. This will help you to develop a strategy for storage and spatial definition to keep potentially warring factions under control.

Storage is not incompatible with style, provided it is well-considered. This wall of books (ABOVE) includes a deep shelf for display to lighten the overall effect.

It often makes good spatial sense to combine living and dining areas (ABOVE RIGHT). Clever furniture arrangement can emphasise the distinction between different activities.

How important is the living room as a place to entertain guests? If your idea of socialising is simply hanging out with old friends, the style of decor should reflect this informality. If, on the other hand, the success of your professional life depends on being able to invite colleagues and clients to your home from time to time, you may need to maintain the living room as a place set somewhat apart from the hurly-burly of family life.

Does your living room serve as the household media centre, complete with television, video, computers and CD player? Is there sufficient storage for tapes, disks and CDs?

Is the living room the main playspace for children? If so, what happens to their toys at the end of the day when it's time for the adults to relax?

Do you need to use the living room as a place for work or quiet study? If so, is it on a regular or an intermittent basis?

Do you intend to eat in the living room, either informally or in a specific dining area?

Do you expect to be able to put guests up overnight in the living room from time to time? Is there a more private space for the sofabed to go?

PLANNING AND ARRANGEMENT

The living room is dominated by various forms of seat furniture, from sofas and armchairs to chaise longues, stools and occasional chairs. Coming up with a good seating arrangement is the key to creating a successful living room with a welcoming and restful atmosphere. Plotting it all out on Graph Paper saves time and effort.

Start by drawing up a scale plan of your living room (see pages 172–73). Then make scale Templates of the furniture you wish to retain, or pieces you intend to buy (see pages 174–77). Moving the pieces about on the plan will give you ideas about optimum arrangement.

An enclosing wall completes a sitting circle arranged around a coffee table. Seats must not be too widely spaced or conversation will be difficult.

A SEATING PLAN

People naturally group themselves in a loose circle when they gather together. Seating that is too widely spaced can be awkward as people will have to raise their voices to talk to one another; similarly, furniture that is arranged in too linear a fashion can also be uncomfortable as people have to twist round to see whom they are addressing.

The classic living room seating plan is enshrined in the traditional three-piece suite: a three-seat sofa, flanked by two matching armchairs. Alternative

Living room arrangements need some kind of focus. French windows provide light and garden views (FAR LEFT); a large rug can be used to anchor furniture arrangement in a generously proportioned space (LEFT); the traditional focus of interest remains the fireplace (BELOW).

arrangements include placing two sofas facing each other or at right angles to each other, with additional armchairs to complete the circle, or using contemporary sectional seating to form a U-shaped enclosure.

In a small room, you will probably need to arrange the bigger pieces of furniture with their backs to walls or windows. If you have more space at your disposal, you can group furniture more centrally in the room, leaving clear floorspace for moving from area to area.

FINDING A FOCUS

Seating plans look more natural when they have a focus – and when that focus is not the television! A fireplace makes a good focal point, with an arrangement of chairs or sofas flanking it on either side. A room that is dominated by a large bay window or French windows can be arranged so that furniture is grouped to make the most of natural light and views. If there isn't an obvious focal point, a feature rug or a coffee table placed centrally can draw the whole arrangement together.

Three into one: reading, relaxing and dining are accommodated in the same area with the use of clever spatial definition (ABOVE). The high-level study area incorporates useful storage space beneath to keep clutter to a minimum, while the dining table is set to one side, away from the main traffic routes.

There is no doubt, however, that one of the main activities that takes place in today's living rooms is watching television. There is little point arranging furniture so that viewing is uncomfortable, but the television can have a very dominating presence. One answer is to place the set on a trolley, which can be wheeled into view when required.

SPATIAL DEFINITION

Marking the boundary between one activity and another is essential if your living room is a multi-purpose space. Without some form of definition, there will be a tendency for all activities to run into each other and your scheme will lack coherence.

A change in level, such as this short flight of steps (ABOVE RIGHT), provides a natural boundary between activities without compromising the light, open quality of the space.

SEPARATE SPACE
The alcove of a bay window can provide a sense of enclosure to make a separate space for a dining table or desk. Similarly, a dining area can be set up at one end of the room in front of a pair of French windows.

The following strategies apply whether you are separating living from dining or working areas, or whether you wish to make a distinction between a formal end of the room and a family-oriented area.

An L-shaped room provides the opportunity to make a natural break between activities. Use the shorter 'leg' of the L-shape for working or dining, activities for which furniture arrangement can be more tightly planned.

If your living room is long and rectangular, think about subdividing it with some form of flexible partition. Double doors fitted in an archway allow you to close off an area if required.

Use a room divider, such as a free-standing storage unit, placed at right angles to the wall to act as a screen between spaces.

Movable folding screens can provide flexible spatial definition.

A change of flooring can help to accentuate a distinction between different areas within a room. For example, if your living room has a wooden floor throughout, a large rug can have a unifying effect for a seating area.

Furniture can be strategically placed to create a sense of separation. A sofa, a line of low cupboards or even a collection of large house-plants can serve as a visual boundary.

LIVING ROOM STYLE

The living room often takes the lion's share of the decorating budget, which is not surprising since its traditional role as the 'best' room in the home is hard for most of us to ignore. But even if you are not bothered about impressing the neighbours, you will probably expect your living room to provide a relatively high degree of comfort: upholstered furniture, such as sofas and armchairs, can amount to rather significant investments. For financial reasons alone, it can be better to opt for classic solutions, period or contemporary, than for a look that may date in a matter of months. This does not mean, however, that your living room needs to be a fashion-free zone. Accents, such as cushion covers and decorative objects, can serve as the accessories in your home's wardrobe, lifting and refreshing a look from season to season.

PROPORTION AND DETAIL

Consider the basic architectural framework of the room: its proportions, features and details, such as fireplaces, decorative plaster mouldings and woodwork. Contemporary living rooms are generally minimally detailed, with lower ceilings and more of a horizontal emphasis, while living rooms in older properties may have high ceilings and a wealth of period features. In general, it is better to work with

Minimally detailed contemporary living rooms allow modern design classics, such as this Egg chair by Danish designer Arne Jacobsen (LEFT), to take centre stage.

A rigorously symmetrical arrangement complements the fine decorative mouldings in this period room (ABOVE RIGHT), making a sympathetic marriage of old and new.

the context, rather than impose a style that is out of keeping with the basic spatial framework. Adding Victorian-style picture rails to a room with modern proportions will look unconvincing because the basic proportions are wrong. In the same way, stripping a period room of all its decorative features is not only tantamount to architectural vandalism, it rarely succeeds in conveying a contemporary atmosphere. Traditional architectural details provide a sense of refinement, but they are not merely decorative flourishes: they perform practical functions.

■ The skirting or baseboard protects the base of the wall from knocks and provides a neat finish where the plane of the wall meets the floor. Victorian and Georgian skirting boards tend to be deeper than contemporary versions.

■ The dado or chair rail is a wooden moulding positioned about one-third of the way up the wall, where a chair back would rest if the chair were pushed back. The function of the dado rail is to protect the wall surface and provide a visually comfortable break in a room with high ceilings.

Large pieces of furniture such as sofas cannot help but dominate a room, which means that it is worth spending time picking the right one. Bear in mind that this is an item that should last a while: avoid eccentric shapes or ultra-fashionable styles that are likely to date very quickly.

■ The picture rail is a wooden moulding set a short way down from the ceiling around the perimeter of the room. It serves as a means of hanging pictures, but it can also signal a break between papered and painted portions of the wall.

■ Cornicing, the decorative plasterwork that runs along the top edge of the wall, has the prosaic function of concealing superficial cracking where one plastered surface meets another.

■ The ceiling rose is positioned centrally in the middle of ceiling as a decorative flourish to mark the presence of a light fitting.

■ The fireplace is the traditional focus of a period home. Styles and materials vary, but it is always best to try to match the surround with its setting.

If you live in a period home that lacks some of its original features, it is easy to restore its historical style. First, undertake some research to establish exactly what type of features might have originally existed. Architectural salvage yards are a good source of fireplaces, mouldings, doors and other architectural features. An alternative is to opt for reproduction features, which are generally cheaper.

CREATING A 'COMFORT ZONE'

The essential function of the living room is to provide comfortable places to sit, which tends to mean at least one sofa and a couple of upholstered chairs. As with all major purchases, it is best to opt for the highest quality you can afford: cheaper furniture will show its age rapidly and need replacing sooner rather than later. Good quality sofas, for example, have sprung bases rather than webbing to support the seating, which makes them both wear better and feel more resilient. Most sofabeds, particularly the type with fold-out mattresses, are more expensive, yet less comfortable than standard sofas. If you need to provide accommodation for occasional overnight guests, a better bet may be roll-up futons that can be stored out of the way when not needed.

If a sofa must look right, it must also feel right. Visit a furniture department or showroom and sit on a selection of sofas to assess their differences. The sofa that is right for your height and build should not leave your back unsupported; it should be deep enough to snuggle up in but not so deep that you can't rest your feet on the floor when sitting upright.

Before you commit yourself to a purchase, ensure that you will be able to get the sofa into the room! Many furniture stores can arrange a home visit to check this out for you in advance.

Think about comfort underfoot. Hard flooring can strike a jarring note in the living room: unless you live in a hot climate, stone, ceramic tile and brick are best avoided without some cushioning element such as a rug or area of matting to domesticate their effect. Loose rugs also soften an expanse of wood flooring and provide colourful accents: make sure these are laid over non-slip matting to prevent accidents. Despite its relative unfashionability, carpet is still many people's

White slip covers (LEFT) reduce
the apparent bulk of large pieces
of furniture.

A pull-up fabric blind provides an
elegant window treatment for a
traditional living room (BELOW).

preferred choice for living room flooring. Wall-to-wall carpeting deadens sound and provides a more restful atmosphere. And for small children, who naturally spend a lot of time playing on the floor, or for those who enjoy kicking off their shoes and sprawling, carpet multiplies the comfort factor enormously.

WINDOW TREATMENTS

Window treatments serve a variety of purposes: they screen views, filter or modulate strong sunlight, provide privacy at night and also serve as draught- or sound-proofing elements.

On the purely decorative front, elaborately draped or tailored curtains work best in classic or traditional rooms; simple gathered styles suit country-style interiors; while fabric or Venetian blinds complement contemporary decor.

▪ If you need privacy and/or light control during the day, screen windows with light, translucent fabric such as fine muslin or lace, combined with heavier outer curtains to draw at night.

▪ Lined curtains are excellent insulators. Choose a coloured lining material for a decorative accent.

▪ Tailored fabric blinds, such as Roman blinds, make an elegant alternative to curtains for period or contemporary schemes.

▪ Sash windows or windows with a vertical rather than horizontal emphasis should be curtained to the floor. Curtains that stop at sill height have an untidy and mean appearance.

▪ A pelmet can add visual height to a room by making a window look taller than it actually is.

▪ For no-sew window effects, attach lengths of fabric to a pole or rod with cafe clips – an excellent way of displaying antique textiles or saris.

LIGHTING

Living rooms tend to be used more frequently during the evening hours, which places a particular emphasis on artificial lighting as a means of generating mood and atmosphere. At the same time, they often accommodate several different activities, which means flexibility is important.

▨ Avoid fixed lighting, such as recessed downlights, which will commit you to a particular furniture arrangement.

▨ Don't rely solely on a central fitting, such as a pendant or chandelier.

▨ Pairs of wall lights, such as sconces or wall-mounted uplights, make good background lighting.

▨ Floor-standing lamps and uplighters add a vertical emphasis and increase the sense of spaciousness.

▨ Table lamps are the mainstay of living room lighting. Coloured shades and decorative bases add visual flair.

▨ Reading or study areas will need a directional task light, positioned so that light falls over your shoulder onto the page or desk.

▨ Use spotlights to accent displays or paintings.

▨ Position a light behind the television or slightly to one side of it to provide a comfortable level of illumination for viewing and to prevent glare from bouncing off the screen.

▨ Use a dimmer switch to provide flexibility of lighting levels.

STORAGE

Living room storage solutions must be as seamless and concealed as possible so as not to undermine the decorative scheme or detract from the general atmosphere of relaxation.

Before you begin to plan storage requirements, review what you are storing and why. It may well be that some of the things you are keeping in the living room could well be housed elsewhere, particularly if these possessions are not needed on a regular basis.

Many living rooms function as the household book and music library, but such collections can devour available space. If you have a wide hallway, lining it with shelves or cupboards can make a practical and attractive solution.

Concealed sources of lighting (LEFT) are both atmospheric and easy on the eyes. Dimmer switches, which enable you to adjust light levels according to the mood or time of day, are invaluable in living areas.

This seating group (RIGHT) is positioned to take full advantage of natural light. The dramatic Arco light, a modern classic designed by Achille Castiglioni in 1962, provides a cosy focus after nightfall.

Fitted storage, built in to the architectural framework of the room, looks elegant and well considered in living areas. The effect is to create 'working walls' that lift clutter from the floor and preserve the sense of spaciousness. Fitted storage can be concealed behind cupboard doors or left out on view, as in the traditional arrangement of library-style shelving. Either way, it should be aligned so that it fits in with existing proportions and detailing.

Unless your storage arrangements are inherently flexible, such as shelving systems that allow you to move the position of shelves up and down a wall-mounted track, you need to consider exactly what you are going to store from the outset. Calculate the length of shelving you need by measuring the amount of space your books, CDs or records occupy and add in a margin for future additions to your collections.

UNFITTED STORAGE

Free-standing cupboards and chests, baskets, trunks and blanket boxes can house a tremendous amount of clutter. Unfitted storage varies widely in design and appearance — from antique armoires to wickerwork hampers or collections of contemporary stacking metal containers — enabling you to choose a style that blends seam-lessly with the rest of your decorative scheme.

▨ Fit shelves into the recesses beside chimney breasts and run them floor to ceiling. Shelves that begin at an indeterminate point halfway up the wall always look like an afterthought.

▨ An entire wall devoted to storage looks better than similar provision dotted around the room.

▨ An arrangement that combines open shelves above a closed cupboard appears more consid-ered if the break between the two comes at a visu-ally comfortable point.

▨ Paint shelves in the same colour as the walls for a seamless look.

▨ Broad wooden battens attached to the front of shelves give them an appearance of solidity.

DISPLAY

Storage and display are intimately related. In the living room, book-lined walls have their own visual appeal. But even if the basic arrangements are similar, displays of favourite objects or personal treasures exist solely to provide delight and decora-tive emphasis. If the purpose of living room storage is to blend in with the background, display is very much about attracting attention.

In the contemporary interior, less is definitely more these days. This does not mean there is no place for collections of objects, merely that they are more effective when grouped so that they read as a whole entity.

▪ Display china and glass on glass shelving, accented by spotlighting for a sparkling effect.

▪ Group objects by theme or colour for added impact.

▪ The mantelpiece – at eye-level – inevitably attracts attention and is ideal for display. Limiting the number of objects adds to the effect.

▪ Position a mirror opposite an open doorway or window to multiply views and increase the sense of light and spaciousness.

▪ Symmetrical arrangements are traditional and classic; asymmetry more challenging and original.

▪ When hanging a collection of pictures, lay them out on the floor or on a tabletop to work out the optimum arrangement. Group pictures by theme or medium.

▪ Fresh flowers provide immediate uplift and vitality. Dried arrangements work best when they are graphic and sculptural, not easy-care versions of the real thing.

An antique pitcher generously filled with flowers makes an ideal display (LEFT).

Varying what you put on show according to mood or season is the easiest way to keep a decorative scheme looking fresh (RIGHT).

DINING AREAS

A sunny conservatory (BELOW) provides a light-filled area for relaxed dining, separate but still connected to the main living space.

The separate dining room (RIGHT) is something of a spatial luxury today.

If the contemporary living room is looking for a function, today's dining rooms are looking for a settled home. No one doubts what a dining area is for, the question is where to locate it?

In the days when children were seen and not heard and women toiled away behind closed doors to produce their family's daily meals, the separate dining room enshrined certain accepted social values. Mealtimes were fixed and invariable and dining was a fairly formal affair, a ritual that punctuated the household routine with the regularity of clockwork. The dining room was the focus for entertaining guests, providing a setting for the display of culinary talents, fine china, cutlery and glassware.

Few aspects of daily life have changed as much as our eating habits. Mealtimes these days are unquestionably more democratic occasions, slotted into busy working schedules, with food prepared quickly and eaten even faster. Where both partners have careers and children have many extra-curricular activities, the opportunities for all members of the family to sit down together may be few and far between. In addition, entertaining has become less about showing off a dinner service and more about creating a relaxed, informal atmosphere. It is small wonder that the separate dining room, which entails to-ing and fro-ing between where the food is cooked and where it is served, has come to be viewed as an anachronism and a spatial luxury.

The disappearance of the dining room may reveal a fundamental shift in values, but it does not mean one has to forego the essential conviviality of eating together. When you sit down with friends or family to enjoy a meal, you are engaging in a fundamental social activity, sharing conversation and companionship as much as food – a snack in front of the television is simply refuelling.

PLANNING AND ARRANGEMENT

There are advantages and disadvantages to every type of dining arrangement and it is unlikely that one particular location will necessarily meet all your requirements. Options to consider include the kitchen-diner and the combined living/dining room. The answer may be to set aside a couple of places where different types of meals can be taken.

SEPARATE DINING ROOM

This arrangement makes sense if your household eats together on a regular, daily basis and if you like to entertain. An advantage is that it promotes togetherness and an exchange of family news and views; a disadvantage is that it can straitjacket your daily routine to an unacceptable degree since mealtimes are invariably less flexible.

A dining area integrated into a kitchen entails less to-ing and fro-ing between where the food is cooked and where it is served. The farmhouse kitchen (RIGHT), with its stone hearth, makes a hospitable setting for family mealtimes.

LIVING/DINING AREAS

Living and eating areas go well together, both spatially and in terms of mood and atmosphere. An eating area in a living room can be dressed more formally for entertaining or simply serve as a place for family get-togethers, while between meals it can usefully double up as a working area.

To work successfully, this arrangement depends on relative proximity to the kitchen – you won't want to traipse up and down flights of stairs to serve food or clear dishes several times a day.

One disadvantage of eating in the living room is that food smells can linger unappetisingly after meals. Soft furnishings, such as carpeting and curtains, which are often desirable in a living area, tend to hold odours.

■ Retain some kind of distinction between the relaxing end of the room and the dining area. (See pages 78–79 for ways of segregating space.)
■ A dining area may require practical flooring that is easy to clean in the event of spills.

COOKING/EATING AREAS

Kitchen-diners make perfect practical sense: food can be served directly from the oven or stove and dishes cleared straight to the sink. Extractor fans clear food smells; surfaces and finishes are likely to be more robust and hence more easily maintained. The natural partnership of cooking and eating makes for an informal atmosphere well attuned to today's relaxed style of entertaining.

A prerequisite is a kitchen that is big enough to accommodate a dining table or a pair of adjacent rooms that can be knocked through to create a kitchen-diner. If you want a central eating area, there must be enough clear space around the table for the cook to work effectively.

The dining area often works when arranged at one end of the room or against one wall.

If your kitchen is quite compact, consider introducing a bar or counter where light meals can be taken, or fit out an alcove with a small table and bench seating.

The main disadvantage to eating in the kitchen is that cooking tends to become something of a performance art. Some people enjoy the social aspects of cooking and welcome company in the kitchen; others find the experience more off-putting.

OPEN PLAN

Living, eating and cooking in the same open-plan space is about as far removed from the formal dining room as it is possible to get. Running activities together makes sense if you live in a small apartment and are short of room: one relatively large area serving all functions is bound to feel more spacious than several tiny ones. Conversely, the arrangement also works well if you have an enormous area to play with – converted lofts and warehouse style apartments and open-plan living go hand in hand.

When all the boundaries are down, living is less formal and more inclusive, which many people view as a positive asset. At the same time, some distinction – decorative or otherwise – is necessary between different areas. The strategies outlined on pages 78–79 can also be employed to provide visual or physical breaks between areas for cooking, eating and relaxing. While the principal drawback of open-plan living is the loss of private space, this tends not to matter when it comes to an essentially social activity, such as eating.

SCREENS
To create a sense of enclosure for the nervous cook, introduce some form of partition between cooking and eating areas. A counter or low run of kitchen units can also help to separate space.

An open divider, used as a means of display (RIGHT), serves to screen a kitchen-diner from the living area.

DINING ROOM STYLE

A dining area is a little like a stage set, coming to life with the performance of each mealtime. But the character of mealtimes varies enormously in most households – from leisurely Sunday breakfasts with the papers, to formal candlelit suppers. In terms of decoration and design, it is important to build in a degree of flexibility to enable you to ring the changes as the need arises. If the background makes a very strong style statement of its own, it can restrict your options.

FURNISHING

First and foremost, dining room furniture should be practical. It is far easier to dress up a basic table for a special occasion than it is to cope with the extra vigilance and maintenance required to keep a beautiful antique in good condition.

In terms of dining, practicality also means sitting comfortably. Dining chairs should provide some support for the back, but need not be highly upholstered. If you prefer upholstered chairs, it is an asset if the covering is removable and washable.

If you are very short of space, folding or stacking chairs can help to keep the floor area clear between meals. Stools and benches are useful for breakfast bars, but they are at best temporary perches and can be tiring if you are sitting at the table for long periods.

■ If entertaining is a priority, choose a table that can be expanded, with pull-out or drop-in leaves, rather than opting for the biggest table you can cram into the room.

■ Ensure there is enough clear space around the table to allow chairs to be pushed back without hitting the walls.

■ Since most rooms are rectangular, rectangular or square tables generally fit the available space better than circular ones, which demand a greater degree of surrounding area.

■ To expand a circular table, borrow a trick from the restaurant business: have a circle of larger diameter cut from a sheet of wood, lay it over the top of your table and dress it with a cloth.

A counter screens kitchen views from the dining area (ABOVE); built-in bench seating makes an economical use of space (RIGHT).

There are many simple, afford-able tables on the market that either resist wear and tear or look all the better for it (LEFT).

SURFACES AND FINISHES

Traditionally, dining rooms were often painted a deep, rich red. It is not hard to see why: red is a celebratory colour that generates a great sense of warmth and intimacy. Red walls may be a little overpowering for today's tastes, but colour can be an important way of giving a dining area its own identity without stealing too much attention from the table. If your dining area is part of a larger space, a change of wall colour can help to emphasise the distinction between different areas. This strategy is often most successful when you introduce 'planes' of colour as spatial markers, picking out just one or two walls.

Restrict soft furnishings to a minimum. Heavy drapery at the window and dense carpeting under-

White roller blinds screen strong light in a dining room (LEFT). Heavy drapery and excessive soft furnishings can hold food smells.

A chandelier, with its many points of shaded light, makes an ideal fitting for a dining area, combining soft, atmospheric light with a sense of theatricality (RIGHT).

foot can hold the smell of cooking. Lighter, or washable window treatments are fresher and more practical; flooring should also be relatively easy to maintain. A suggestion of comfort can be provided by a large area rug placed under the dining table, but ensure that it is easy to clean.

LIGHTING

No single factor is more important when it comes to creating dining room style than lighting. Atmospheric lighting contributes immeasurably to the pleasure of dining, drawing people together in the same cosy circle.

A dining area obviously requires lighting that is focused on the table itself. But some background lighting is also essential; without it, there will be too great a contrast of light levels in the room and the consequent risk of glare. If possible, all dining area lighting should be dim-able to enable you to adjust the mood according to the occasion.

Background lighting for dining areas is usefully provided by wall lights in some form or other. Wall-mounted shaded sconces or shallow dished uplights are discreet and unobtrusive. Alternatively, you could position a series of table lamps around the room on sideboards or storage units.

If you are confident that your dining table is going to remain in the same position, fixed lighting arrangements, such as small angled spotlights and recessed downlights, can provide attractive solutions to lighting the table. Positioning is critical to avoid glare or harshness of effect.

A mirror or pair of mirrors placed opposite each other can add vitality and a sense of theatre to your lighting arrangements, particularly in dining areas. And don't forget candles – the soft glow of candlelight is the most flattering, intimate and atmospheric light of all.

■ A pendant is a popular option for lighting the table. It directs light downward, where it is gently reflected from the table, crockery and glassware onto the faces of diners.

■ Ensure that pendant lights are hung at the right level. If hung too high, light will shine uncomfortably in people's eyes; if it is too low, it will interfere with views across the table.

■ Avoid glare by choosing a pendant that either conceals the light source completely or diffuses it.

■ A long refectory style table may require a series of pendants to light its length.

A sideboard (LEFT) provides traditional storage space for the accessories of dining.

Storage meets display in this arrangement of plain white serving dishes (RIGHT).

It makes sense to keep cutlery, crockery, glassware and table linen close to where they are going to be used (FAR RIGHT).

STORAGE TIPS

Stack small plates or bowls according to size and pattern to make retrieval easy. Store plates upright in a plate rack to avoid chipping or damaging glazed finishes. Nest cups in small groups lying on their sides. Never hang them up by their handles.

STORAGE

Traditional dining room storage pieces, such as sideboards or dressers, provide surfaces for serving or display. But dining areas in contemporary homes can be compact, which means that there is a good argument for keeping such furnishing to a minimum. If space is at a premium, you may have to rely on storage in an adjacent area, such as a kitchen.

■ Stemmed glasses should be stored upright, not resting on their rims.

■ Fine china services that are used infrequently can be stored in protective felt bags.

■ Invest in a drawer divider to organise cutlery.

■ Silverware tarnishes if exposed to light and humidity. Store dishes in felt bags; store cutlery in felt-lined canteens.

A toile de Jouy tablecloth harmonises with red and white crockery in this traditional French dining room.

DRESSING THE TABLE

The advantages of keeping basic decor simple in dining areas is particularly apparent when it comes to putting on a show for a special occasion. With a relatively restrained background, a well-dressed table will have that much more impact.

For sheer simplicity and elegance, it is hard to beat a plain white cloth and white china (RIGHT).

- Reflective materials – silverware, glasses and crystal, glazed china – catch the light and add sparkle to tabletop displays.
- Brightly coloured or patterned table linen can be very attractive, but it is hard to beat plain white damask for style and luxury.

- Arrange seasonal fruit on generous coloured platters to make eye-catching and appetising centrepieces.
- Small floating candles or nightlights individualise place settings.
- Don't overdo table decoration: simplicity is best.

KITCHENS

No single area in the modern home works harder than the kitchen. It is not that we are spending more time cooking meals – in fact, statistics show that the amount of time the average person devotes to cooking and food preparation has dropped dramatically in recent years. But if less in the way of hard work actually takes place in the kitchen, it has come to assume a new role as the unofficial heart of the home. Increasingly we eat in the kitchen, entertain in the kitchen, pay bills, do homework and even relax in the kitchen – a multiplicity of functions that can impose heavy demands on any space no matter what its size.

Hand in hand with the concept of living in the kitchen has gone an increasing interest in kitchen style and decoration. Today, kitchen fittings and fixtures are big business and a host of different looks are heavily marketed: everything from country-style kitchens, complete with terracotta-tiled floors, scrubbed oak units and the obligatory Aga, to gleaming stainless steel laboratories of high cuisine accessorised with the latest designer gadgets.

Style is fun and the old-fashioned kitchen, which always scored higher on practicality than it ever did on visual appeal, was certainly ripe for a makeover. Nevertheless, the kitchen is one area where functional matters must take precedence. A kitchen that is beautifully decorated but a nightmare to work in causes a very special kind of daily frustration and annoyance. Whatever your decorative taste, it is essential to get the basic layout right, which means careful planning.

The professional kitchen (LEFT and RIGHT) is a source of reference for domestic design.

ASSESSING YOUR NEEDS

Before you begin, spend some time thinking about how you actually use the kitchen. Much will depend on your particular lifestyle, whether or not you entertain and whether or not you positively like to cook. Note the replies in your Notebook.

■ Do you value cooking as a means of creativity? Are you always experimenting with new techniques and ingredients?

■ How often do you cook for family or friends?

■ Are there any other cooks in your household? Do you like to share cooking activities or do you prefer to work on your own?

■ How often do you shop? Do you need a freezer or extensive storage for bulk purchases or do you shop more casually and frequently?

■ Does the kitchen function as the household nerve centre? Is there space to carry out basic administration, such as take messages or do paperwork?

The layout of this kitchen-diner (LEFT) provides a degree of separation between the two activities. A compact fitted kitchen (RIGHT) makes the most of available wall space and incorporates a breakfast bar at the end of the counter.

■ Do you eat in the kitchen? Do you need to provide storage in the kitchen for dishes, tablelinen and tableware?

■ Do you enjoy eating outside? Does the kitchen provide ready access to outdoor areas?

■ What other activities take place in the kitchen on a regular basis: laundry, play, homework, entertaining, visits from friends?

Answers to the preceding questions should reveal some sort of pattern. If you live alone and cooking elaborate meals currently ranks fairly low on your list of priorities, a compact kitchen area that is easy to maintain would fit the bill. If, on the other hand, you have a growing family to feed and supervise, you will need generous amounts of space for preparing meals, storage and accommodating other activities. If your household falls somewhere between these two extremes, you might think about increasing the degree of flexibility in your kitchen arrangements, by creating connections with other areas in the home, for example.

PLANNING AND ARRANGEMENT

The dream kitchen of popular imagination is always exceptionally spacious, but when it comes to kitchen layout, size is not everything. In fact, there are good arguments in favour of small kitchens where everything is at hand and distances between preparation and cooking areas are as short as possible. Size alone does not make a perfect kitchen, but good planning does: drawing up a detailed floor plan will save you a great deal of time and expense later on in the design process.

A hundred years ago or more, when domestic work was largely undertaken by servants and the mistress of the house visited the kitchen only rarely to instruct her cook, no one paid much attention to the finer points of kitchen organisation. But in succeeding decades, social conditions changed and wives and mothers increasingly found themselves solely responsible for providing all their families' meals. In the wake of such change, and with the advent of new technology, attempts were made to analyse the sequence of work in the domestic

Clear, short routes between the main centres of kitchen activity (LEFT) save time and increase efficiency. Acres of work surface and a refrigerator the size of a small room may be many people's ideal, but large kitchens can be tiring places to work (RIGHT).

kitchen in order to rationalise planning and improve conditions. These ergonomic studies still form the basis for kitchen planning today.

WORK TRIANGLE

Good kitchen planning is founded on the principle of the 'work triangle', which is the essential relationship between the sink, the refrigerator and the oven or stove – or in other words between wet, cold and hot areas. Kitchens function best when the distances between each point in the 'triangle' are not too great: the recommended overall distance is about 6 metres (20ft).

The work triangle compresses the bulk of kitchen activity into a tight focus but, at the same time, the focus must not be too tight or the kitchen will feel cramped and awkward. You will need adequate counter space between areas to work effectively, set down pots and pans, and prepare fresh food. For practical reasons it is also a good idea if the refrigerator is sited away from the immediate vicinity of the stove and oven.

A wider-than-average galley layout (ABOVE) allows space for a narrow island, which doubles as a preparation and extra storage area.

With the work triangle as your starting point, there are a number of options for kitchen layouts, which depend on the amount of space at your disposal and its basic shape. Use the Graph Paper and Templates to test different combinations. Both 'white goods' – refrigerators, dishwashers, washing machines, stoves and freezers – and fitted kitchen units generally conform to the same basic dimensions, with most appliances and base units being variations on a 600mm (2ft) module.

In-line layouts arrange the sink and all the main appliances along the length of a wall. Such designs look neat and well organised, but if the distances are great they can be tiring to work in.

L-shaped layouts make use of two flanking walls, pivoting work surfaces and built-in features at the right angle.

U-shaped layouts are extremely workable, not least because they maximise the amount of area devoted to preparation.

Galley layouts are particularly suitable for narrow, confined spaces that are designed for single cooks.

Island layouts group at least some of the kitchen functions at a central workstation, with walls devoted principally to storage. This type of arrangement is ideal for the sociable cook, but you need plenty of space.

Very small kitchens call for precision planning. Here (ABOVE) an in-line arrangement is the most practical solution, with a narrow counter providing a space for eating light meals.

U-shaped layouts are extremely practical and make efficient working environments. In this case (LEFT), one arm of the U serves as a screen for the dining area beyond.

KITCHEN STYLE

Kitchen style is dominated by the way in which the equipment and paraphernalia essential to the preparation and cooking of food is organised. To begin with, you should decide whether you want your kitchen to be fitted or unfitted. While most kitchens contain at least some elements of both types of arrangement, the emphasis is bound to fall on one side or the other.

In the postwar period, the fitted kitchen was the epitome of modern luxury. Today, the pendulum has swung in the opposite direction and unfitted kitchens, complete with butcher's blocks, dressers and other free-standing storage pieces, are the height of chic. While the unfitted kitchen often has nostalgic overtones, some contemporary kitchen manufacturers also market industrial style workstations with a decidedly high-tech appearance.

The ultimate fitted kitchen (LEFT), finished in stainless steel, makes a strong style statement.

A spacious farmhouse kitchen (RIGHT), complete with Aga set into the hearth, is furnished with a variety of traditional free-standing storage pieces.

The principal advantage of the unfitted kitchen is that it is portable: you can take your investment with you when you move. There's also a greater degree of flexibility: while you certainly would not want to shift a hefty dresser around at whim, there are many small pieces on the market, many on castors, that can be wheeled around as needed. Fitted kitchens, on the other hand, commit you to a fixed arrangement, but with optimum planning they can represent a more efficient use of space.

If your kitchen is looking a little tired, consider changing the doors or drawer fronts of units. Most built-in kitchens are produced to the same basic dimensions and the underlying frameworks or 'carcasses' are broadly similar, so the substitution is an easy one to make.

Replacing cheap laminate doors with ones made of solid wood can radically transform the look of your kitchen at a fraction of the cost of buying a new one.

STORAGE

To a large degree, storage is what a kitchen is all about. We keep a great number of items in the kitchen, items which may differ widely not only in size, shape and type but also in the type of storage conditions they require. In other areas of the home, poor organisation may simply be a source of minor muddle and aggravation. In the kitchen, however, it can more crucially be a matter of sickness or health. Food that is kept in improper conditions can deteriorate rapidly, increasing the risk of illness.

The other key aspect of kitchen organisation is that it must be tailored to everyday procedures and activities. Utensils on daily call must be stored so they can be reached without a moment's thought.

■ Cupboards and fitted units with adjustable shelving make good practical sense. Arrange foodstuffs and kitchen equipment by size and shape.

■ Sliding doors take up less space than hinged doors that open out.

■ Glazed-fronted wall units are less dominating than those with solid doors.

■ Pull-out basket shelves make it easier to get access to ingredients and prevent small items from being overlooked.

■ If the legs of base units are exposed, rather than concealed behind a plinth, the overall effect is lighter and more spacious-looking.

■ Update cupboard doors with a fresh coat of paint and new handles.

Wall-hung glass-fronted cupboards over fitted cupboards echo the design of the traditional kitchen dresser (LEFT). A tiered stand is a good way of organising pots and pans.

Retro-style kitchen equipment, such as this huge 1950s refrigerator and the weighing scales, often function every bit as well as the latest technology.

STORING FOOD

■ Keep canned food in a cool, clean, dry cupboard, arranged so that you use the oldest of any multiple first.

■ Store staple provisions, such as rice, flour, sugar or pulses, in matching canisters or containers with airtight lids.

■ Herbs and spices lose their bite and flavour if kept too long. Buy in small quantities and store in airtight containers. Only keep those you use most frequently on a wall rack or open shelf: most spices keep better in dark, cool conditions.

■ Wine is best stored lying on its side in a wine rack in a cool location.

STORING EQUIPMENT AND UTENSILS

■ Cast a critical eye over your kitchen equipment and evaluate which dishes, gadgets or utensils you actually use on a regular basis. If you use a food processor every day, award it counter space; if you use it once a year, it probably shouldn't be in the kitchen at all.

■ Store kitchen knives separately in a slotted knife box or on a wall-mounted magnetic strip.

■ Wall racks near cooking and preparation areas are good for storing basic utensils in everyday use.

■ Nest pots and pans and store lids separately to save space.

Kitchenalia does not necessarily need to be hidden away behind closed doors. Robust open shelving keeps everything on view (ABOVE).

Suspend utensils that are in frequent use from a rack or rail next to the preparation area (LEFT).

Gleaming stainless steel and glass brick have a contemporary edge (RIGHT), but they will show every fingermark!

SURFACES AND FINISHES

Kitchens are pretty extreme environments that demand a robust approach when it comes to decoration. Surfaces and finishes must be tough enough to take a fair amount of punishment, yet easy to keep clean and hygienic. Such considerations, however, do not mean you have to sacrifice all thoughts of style. Evocative contrasts of material

– for example, wood and terracotta, glass and metal, stone and ceramic tile – can be employed to create decorative schemes that are as dynamic as they are functional.

There is a huge range of options for countertops and work surfaces: choice of material is not only dependent on practicality, but also provides the opportunity to introduce textural interest.

■ The cheapest work surfaces are synthetic. Many designs simulate real materials, some more successfully than others. An advantage is that maintenance is generally trouble-free.

■ Solid wood worktops are generally made of a hardwood, such as iroko. Choose oiled worktops rather than lacquered varieties, which are less hard wearing and prone to damage.

■ Granite work surfaces are expensive, but extremely hard wearing. Black granite has a sleek, contemporary look.

■ A marble slab inset into the worktop provides an ideal surface for rolling pastry.

■ Tiled worktops are practical and economical. Match tiles with the wall colour or add a pattern or colour accent.

■ Steel surfaces are the ultimate in modernity, but require extra vigilance to stay looking good.

A fully tiled splashback makes a practical surface for the wall behind the sink (LEFT). Alcove shelving has been finished with broad beading on the leading edges for an impression of greater solidity.

Sealed raw plaster and pale natural wood (RIGHT) make a rustic combination, full of textural variety.

WALLS

As kitchens tend to be rather busy environments, with a lot of visual detail, there is a good argument for keeping basic decoration fairly simple, painting walls in solid colour rather than adopting a more elaborately patterned scheme. Warm rich tones, such as terracotta and golden yellows, make a good backdrop for country-style fixtures and fittings; cool blues are refreshing and inherently domestic-looking. For a vivid contemporary style, acid shades of lime, orange or shocking pink can make dramatic accents when used to pick out a wall.

Some manufacturers produce paint specifically designed for kitchen use that is more resistant to changes in humidity and easier to wipe clean if accidentally splashed with grease. In any case, wall areas behind the sink and stove will need additional protection in the form of splashbacks. A splashback can be chosen so that it blends in with the overall decoration, or used as a means of making a graphic contrast of colour or material.

▪ For a neat, finished look, match the splashback with the work surface or countertop.
▪ Sheets of toughened glass or acrylic screwed into position provide visual continuity.

Wooden flooring (LEFT) is easy to maintain and is more resilient and more comfortable than harder types of flooring.

A beautiful slate floor adds distinction to this kitchen (ABOVE). Stone floors require professional laying.

WINDOWS

Soft furnishings are best kept to a minimum in the kitchen. Choose sill-length curtains in a washable fabric and a plain heading style. In the case of windows that are positioned near stoves, curtains should be avoided altogether to prevent the risk of fire. Fabric, metal or wooden slatted blinds make good-looking and practical alternatives.

FLOORING

Kitchen floors need to be extremely hard wearing and easy to keep clean, which tends to rule out softer flooring options such as carpet and natural fibres. Very hard floors, however, such as stone and brick, can be tiring if you are standing for long periods of time and have the added disadvantage that you will definitely break whatever you drop onto them. Make sure that kitchen flooring is non-slip to avoid accidents.

Wood flooring – sanded and polished floor-boards, laminate or solid hardwood – is clean-lined and sympathetic for most decorative styles.

Suitable stone flooring includes slate, limestone and terrazzo, an aggregate of marble chips and concrete.

Terracotta tiles add a homely, domestic quality. There is a huge range on offer, from handmade traditional tiles to machine-produced quarries.

Ceramic tiles have a crisp, contemporary look. Choose a matt surface to prevent slipping.

Rubber, linoleum and vinyl come in either sheet or tile format and in a wide range of colours and patterns. Linoleum makes a particularly good kitchen floor due to its anti-bacterial properties.

LIGHTING

As kitchens have changed into areas in which we positively want to spend time, the style of lighting has become much more hospitable and atmospheric. Nevertheless, the starting point with any kitchen lighting scheme is function and practicality. Wielding sharp knives and performing any one of a number of procedures that might involve boiling water, scalding steam or sizzling oil, are not activities to be carried out in conditions of relative darkness. Glare is just as hazardous in such circumstances as hardly being able to see at all. The

main preparation and cooking areas in the kitchen need to be well lit, both in terms of light levels and positioning. Such task lighting must be related to the basic kitchen layout so that you are not working in your own shadow. In most cases, this means arranging lighting so that it shines directly onto the work surface.

Most kitchens are fitted in some way; if they are not entirely built-in, at least the main points of servicing will be fixed. For this reason, fixed lighting systems are eminently practical: mounted or recessed spotlights, downlights or concealed strips.

A sequence of small pendants light a breakfast bar and kitchen counter (LEFT). This arrangement (RIGHT), with downlights supplemented by strip lights concealed at the base of wall units, marries efficiency with aesthetics.

■ For background or ambient light, use wall-mounted spots or uplighters, or tube lights concealed behind the cornicing of wall units to direct light up and reflect from the ceiling.

■ Task lighting can be supplied by downlighters positioned over the work surface, wall- or ceiling-mounted directional spots or by strip lighting installed behind a baffle at the base of wall units.

■ Spotlights on concertina arms make flexible task-lighting when clipped to the edge of a shelf or to a metal rail.

■ Additional task lighting can be supplied by integral lights in stove hoods or extractor fans. Interior lights triggered when you open the door can be useful for large food cupboards or walk-in larders.

■ Pay attention to the quality of the light source. Low voltage halogen, with its crisp white light, represents colour well, which is an advantage in food preparation.

■ Fit a dimmer switch if the kitchen is part of a multi-purpose space to enable you to change the mood in an instant.

BEDROOMS

The bedroom is where we spend roughly one-third of our lives. Admittedly, for much of that time we are asleep, but even so the bedroom's importance as a personal space or place of refuge cannot be underestimated. Because bedrooms are largely private places, there can be the temptation to ignore them, decoratively speaking, and devote greater efforts and more of your available budget to improvements elsewhere in the home, where such changes are more likely to be seen and appreciated. But this approach is somewhat shortsighted. The room where you begin and end the day can have a critical impact on your sense of well-being.

When you are winding down or waking up to new challenges, you tend to be more aware of your surroundings. Try to make the bedroom as pleasant a place as it can be.

Qualities such as the levels of light, sound and temperature and all the other factors that promote physical and psychological ease are important in any area in the home. However, it is in the bedroom that we are most likely to notice and become irritated by what are even minor deficiencies. For reasons of comfort alone, it is worth spending time and effort making your bedroom as pleasant a place as it can be.

The bedroom may be defined by the largest and most important piece of furniture it contains, but it is likely to serve other functions as well. Most of us keep the majority of our clothing and personal accessories in our bedrooms; in some homes bedrooms serve as mini-entertainment zones or even places of work.

The multi-purpose bedroom is a particular feature of childhood, where sleep, play, homework and entertainment compete for space, all against a time frame in which these interests and activities are constantly evolving and changing. As the child matures into a young adult, the bedroom inevitably becomes the focus for decorative experiment and self-expression, not to mention a battleground!

ASSESSING YOUR NEEDS

As with any area in the home, it is worth making a preliminary assessment of your needs to determine the best use of the available space. The average family home generally offers a choice of bedrooms, a factor that is particularly relevant when it comes to deciding which room to adopt as the main bedroom and which to allocate to the children.

Traditionally, the 'master' bedroom has tended to be the largest or larger of the available options, with the smaller rooms being earmarked for the children, but this convention is founded more on an outmoded notion of hierarchy than strict common sense. Children may be smaller than adults, but they actually require more space, particularly in the early years. A large room shared by siblings can function as a playroom as well as a bedroom, keeping mayhem in other living areas down to an acceptable level.

Similarly, you may wish to look at adjacent areas such as bathrooms or hallways with a view to creating a separate dressing area. This strategy can dramatically reduce bedroom clutter and help to create a more relaxing atmosphere.

Then there are issues to do with orientation and privacy, where personal tastes come into play.

An adjoining dressing area, where clothes are stored (LEFT), allows the bedroom to remain a peaceful refuge.

Some people like to be woken with the light, others cannot sleep unless there are conditions of total blackout. Some individuals can sleep through a riot, others are disturbed by the slightest noise. Choosing the room where the basic conditions provide the right context for your sleeping pattern is half the battle when it comes to creating a sympathetic and comfortable environment.

Bedrooms can serve as useful daytime retreats, too. Here (ABOVE) a window seat provides space for reading or simply daydreaming.

PLANNING AND ARRANGEMENT

The position of the bed is obviously the key factor in bedroom arrangement. Finding the optimum position is a question of not only practicality, but also psychological comfort. Some arrangements might be perfectly adequate from the point of view of spatial planning yet simply not 'feel' right. for example, most people instinctively feel more comfortable and secure when they can see the bedroom door from their bed.

In terms of basic practicality, it is often more comfortable if the bed is placed between a window and a radiator to benefit from natural ventilation and avoid extremes of temperature. For ease of bedmaking, the bed should be positioned so that only the head is against a wall, leaving clear space round the remaining three sides; children, however, often enjoy the sense of security that comes from having beds aligned along a wall.

Plot different arrangements on Graph Paper and sketch in possible storage solutions if you intend to house your entire wardrobe in the same room. At this point, you should also consider the position of electrical sockets and light switches. You will need points near the bedside for reading lamps; it is often a good idea to be able to control any central or background lighting from the bed to prevent you from having to fumble around in the dark.

The alcoves to either side of a chimney breast are ideal places for fitted or hanging storage (FAR RIGHT).

Seamless cupboards on press catches (RIGHT) turn the entire bedroom into a fitted room.

STORAGE

Neat, integrated storage for clothing, accessories and personal belongings is essential if the bedroom is not to be overrun by clutter. Traditional free-standing storage pieces are generally fairly bulky and can devour floor space. Shelves and hanging rails fitted into alcoves or along the length of the wall often make a better use of space. Such fitted arrangements must blend in with the architectural character of the room, otherwise the result will look like an uncomfortable afterthought.

Before you begin to plan your storage require-ments weed out the has-beens from your wardrobe: you may need less storage space than you think!

■ Fit two rails one above the other to maximise space and group clothes by length and type.

■ Allow a depth of at least 600mm (2ft) for hanging space.

■ Folded clothes can be stored in drawers, sliding trays, pull-out baskets or on shelves. Don't fill drawers more than two-thirds of their depth.

■ Sliding doors, pull down blinds and fixed shelving are more space-saving than hinged doors or drawers that pull out.

■ Think laterally: redundant shop fittings and display cabinets, trolleys, school trunks, baskets and hampers can all be pressed into service to organise your wardrobe.

CHOOSING A BED

A bed may not be the most exciting of purchases, but it is one of the most important. In fact, it is the mattress that is the truly critical part of the equation and which determines whether or not you will have a good night's sleep. Buy the best you can afford and research the market thoroughly so that you choose the one which best supports your physique and sleeping habits.

People have different preferences when it comes to the degree of hardness or softness of a mattress, but there are certain guidelines to bear in mind when making your selection.

■ The best mattresses are constructed of individual springs set into pockets that provide support wherever pressure is applied.

■ In mattresses that have continuous springs, the denser the springs the better the support will be.

■ A mattress should support each person's weight independently.

■ Foam mattresses are designed to be used with sprung bed bases and do not last as long as sprung mattresses.

■ Choose a mattress that is covered with natural fibres that 'breathe' and absorb moisture better.

The framework of the bed, the bedstead or bed base, essentially plays a supporting role to the mattress. Whereas mattresses need replacing after about ten years' continuous use, the bed itself can last a lifetime or more. There is a huge number of designs on the market, from elaborate four-poster affairs to discreet divans.

It is important to choose the right mattress for your weight and frame. If the mattress is too soft, you will sink into a fixed position; if it is too hard you will be forced to lie unnaturally straight.

Four-posters or curtained beds (RIGHT) provide a comforting sense of enclosure, a room within a room.

■ If you are short of space, a bed base that incorporates drawers can provide room to store bulky sweaters, blankets, bedlinen or shoes.

■ Beds with hangings – such as tented beds or four-posters – have great romantic appeal. The sense of enclosure that they provide can be welcome if the bedroom is very spacious.

■ You can create the suggestion of a headboard by hanging a section of carved panelling, a rug or an embroidered textile at the head of the bed.

■ Antique and secondhand shops are good sources of Victorian brass bedsteads, 'sleigh' beds and other period pieces. Some modern manufacturers also produce convincing reproductions.

BEDROOM STYLE

Bedrooms have traditionally been decorated in what, for the want of a better term, might be called a 'feminine' way, with soft colours, flowery patterns and plenty of flounces. But it can be somewhat emasculating for male partners to spend what is after all a large portion of their lives in a relentlessly frilly environment. If you are single, you can obviously please yourself and choose how far to go down the boudoir route; if setting up home with another person, the bedroom you share should endeavour to reflect both of your tastes.

WALLS

The bedroom's decorative scheme is particularly dependent on the quality of light. Go for warm, sunny colours if the bedroom is relatively dark or faces north; cooler, more distancing shades are fresh and airy in rooms with plenty of direct light or a southerly aspect. Pink and green makes a pretty, countrified combination – restful and soothing without being dull. Very strong or rich colours can be used successfully particularly if the room is fairly dark anyway, but such shades need handling with care or the result can be too stimulating.

An antique cast-iron bedstead makes a sympathetic choice for a country cottage bedroom (LEFT), with its half-timbered distempered walls.

Jute matting laid over parquet adds a layer of softness underfoot (RIGHT). Jute is the lightest and most comfortable of all the natural fibres.

Patterned walls call for a similar element of restraint. Very dense or busy prints can be distracting and a trifle claustrophobic, especially where the design is repeated or coordinated on bedlinen or curtains. Simple sprigged floral patterns can be fresh and charming; textured papers, such as Japanese grass papers, have an Eastern feel.

FLOORING

Comfort underfoot is essential in the bedroom which, after all, is one place where we are almost certain to be barefooted part of the time.

■ Lighter weights of carpeting are appropriate here. Special underlay is available for increasing sound insulation, if noise is a problem.

■ Alternatives to carpet include the range of natural fibre coverings, which are available in wall-to-wall formats. Sisal, seagrass and jute are the most appropriate choices for bedroom use.

■ For asthma sufferers or those who prefer more of a clean-lined look, wood makes a practical and attractive flooring option.

■ Flatweave runners can be used around the bed to provide a colourful and comfortable pathway.

SOFT FURNISHINGS

Fabric treatments – from throws and counterpanes to curtains and blinds – soften the look of the room and add to the sense of comfort and relaxation.

■ Synthetic fibres may promise easy-care, but natural materials are infinitely more pleasant next to the skin. Egyptian cotton sheets are luxurious.

■ Dress the bed with patchwork quilts, blankets or throws in deep rich colours, or handprinted textiles for a layered look.

■ Drape a length of fine muslin or mosquito netting over a hoop suspended from the ceiling for an instant tented bed.

■ Line curtains with blackout lining if you prefer to sleep in conditions of total darkness.

BEDSIDE LIGHTS

Each side of the bed should have its own reading lamp. Angled lights that can be directed to shine on the page are most practical. If you do not have space for bedside tables, there are various designs of task light that can be wall-mounted.

Vivid throws and antique textiles (LEFT) add colour accents and warmth. Adjustable Venetian blinds and lined curtains (ABOVE) provide optimum light control.

Marble floor tiles create a graphic pathway to an adjoining bathroom (RIGHT).

LIGHTING

Poor lighting in the bedroom will undermine all your best decorative efforts. To maintain an atmosphere of relaxation, lighting should be subtle and soothing.

■ Avoid central light fittings if at all possible. Not only do they serve to deaden the relaxing mood, they are also right in your eyeline when you are lying in bed.

■ Provide background lighting with table lamps or wall-mounted fittings.

■ A dimmer switch enables you to adjust the mood and atmosphere according to the time of day.

CHILDREN'S ROOMS

The bedroom assumes the status of a world in miniature where children are concerned. Children often become very attached to their rooms, which represent security and their own sense of ownership. The difficulty, where parents are concerned, is keeping abreast of the many changes and stages as the child grows from baby, toddler and school child into the years of young adulthood. A certain degree of flexibility is important to keep pace with the rate of change, but each developmental stage brings its own specific requirements.

NURSERY

The imminent arrival of a new family member has a tendency to bring out the nesting instinct with a vengeance. For those on the brink of parenthood, tiny nursery furniture and wallpaper, borders and friezes patterned with bunnies and ducks tug at the heartstrings, but it is important to remember that they also tug at the purse-strings. As many parents soon discover, babies prefer to be as close to them as possible for much of the day (and night), which may mean that the nursery only begins to come into its own later on.

The stuff of every little girl's dreams – a fairy-tale bed tented with fine net (LEFT). Even very young babies are stimulated by bright colour and strong shapes. Bold patterned borders and friezes (ABOVE RIGHT) provide interest at an early stage of development.

▨ Keep backgrounds simple. Painted walls can be redecorated and retouched more readily than papered walls.

▨ Small, rather than miniaturised, furniture represents a better investment. Tiny nursery pieces will be quickly outgrown.

▨ A low armless nursing chair is invaluable if you are breastfeeding your child.

▨ In the early months, a chest can provide a place to keep linen, shawls, nappies and other nursing essentials.

▨ Store toys in a basket, toy box or similar container that can be moved from place to place.

▨ Soft flooring such as low pile carpeting is kind to tender young knees.

SAFETY

When the baby starts to become mobile, which happens terrifyingly quickly, the whole issue of safety becomes of prime concern. Careful planning and forethought can help to prevent accidents.

▨ Table lamps must be properly secured so that they cannot be tugged over onto the floor. Keep flexes and switches well out of reach. Sockets should be covered.

▨ Shield sharp corners and edges with corner guards.

▨ Provide light control in the form of blinds or sill-length curtains. Curtains that reach the floor can tempt toddlers to engage in indoor mountaineering.

Bed, storage and desk space in one, this fitted unit (LEFT) maximises space for play. Older children and teenagers need both privacy and the opportunity to express their own emerging ideas about style (BELOW and RIGHT).

THE SCHOOL-AGE CHILD

By the time your child reaches school age, he or she will have accumulated a great many possessions – and there may be new siblings to take into the equation as well. Good organisation is critical to keep an element of control over the situation and to prevent endless bickering where children share a room and endlessly dispute property rights.

▪ Place shelves and rails at a height that can easily be reached by the child.

▪ Organise toys, puzzles and games by type in a series of different containers. Plastic stacking boxes help to systemise storage: alternatives include old shoe boxes, baskets, string bags and similar types of improvised container.

▪ Bunk beds appeal to most children, but are unsuitable for the very young. Make sure there is a sturdy, well-anchored ladder, that the basic framework is stable and strong, and that the upper bunk has guard rails.

▪ Provide plenty of space for display. Children like to keep their artwork, favourite toys and special treasures in full view.

▪ Provide an area for quiet study. A desk and task light help to promote good work habits. If space is short, you might consider the option of a platform or high-level bed with a study area underneath.

THE TEENAGER

Teenagers need privacy and the opportunity to exercise at least some control over their surroundings. Teenage rebellion can take many forms, but the most common and, chronologically speaking the earliest manifestation, is the bedroom from hell. For some, it is the insistence on a black, purple or dayglo colour scheme; for others it is the mouldering layer of clothing covering the floor. What such preferences have in common is the need to reach beyond the family for a sense of identity.

To survive these years you need less of a decorating strategy than a coping strategy. Try to provide a framework that addresses specific needs.

Walls of built-in shelving offer the potential to keep clutter under control. Most teenagers' possessions, from books and magazines to CDs, disks and tapes, are readily shelved.

Line a whole wall with cork or provide a really large noticeboard for the inevitable collage.

Underbed storage, such as low boxes on castors, is ideal for sports equipment.

Filing cabinets that slot under desks provide a place to keep schoolwork, makeup or accessories.

Go along with the fun. Whether it's a lava lamp, an inflatable armchair or a glitter ball, teenagers all have their own objects of desire. It may not be your taste but – for the moment – it's theirs.

BATHROOMS

In recent years, just as the kitchen has taken on the role of an informal living area, the bathroom has shrugged off its utilitarian image to emerge as something of a personal sanctuary. Today, we take the functional side of matters for granted; what is increasingly required is a room where our senses can be soothed and refreshed. This entails treating the bathroom as a room in its own right, rather than merely the location where the necessary fittings and fixtures are conveniently installed.

Tongue-and-groove panelling (ABOVE) combines charm with practicality, while a giant free-standing tub (RIGHT) turns a room into a temple of bathing.

The bathroom itself has a relatively short history, only appearing as a standard, internal domestic feature around the beginning of the last century. While North America has always been more advanced in this respect, in Britain outdoor 'privies' and tin baths in front of the fire were by no means uncommon up until the Second World War. Although early bathrooms in wealthy households could be grand affairs, most were far from pleasant places to linger, a fact that was only compounded by the coyness and embarrassment with which most people viewed the entire subject. Euphemisms such as 'the smallest room' or 'the powder room' revealed an innate squeamishness that stood in the way of a more positive approach to bathroom decor and design.

Thankfully, times have changed. Looking after one's body has become more of a sensual affair than the necessary exercise of personal hygiene. The restorative effects of hot, scented baths and skin-tingling showers that wash away the cares and stresses of modern life, rank in equal importance to the basic need to keep clean. The room where these activities are carried out puts us in touch with such elemental pleasures.

PLANNING AND ARRANGEMENT

As with any essentially fitted room, planning and layout are of supreme importance. While the bathroom is no longer inevitably 'the smallest room' most are less generously proportioned than other areas in the home, particularly those in period properties. If space is very tight, a few inches in either direction can make the difference between a room that is workable and one that is not.

The ideal bathroom layout should provide some separation of activities, so that bathing and washing are not carried out in too close proximity to the lavatory. A half-width partition can be used as a screen between the two areas, or you can arrange matters so that there is a completely separate lavatory or shower room.

Large bathrooms allow a certain separation of activities and offer more possibilities when it comes to layout (FAR LEFT). If you have space, bath-tubs set at right angles to the wall (LEFT) make for a more dynamic arrangement.

Bigger bathrooms provide a better opportunity for self-indulgence and pampering, as well as space for chairs, chests and other pieces that contribute to a furnished rather than clinical look. But it is also worth remembering that if a bathroom is very large, the effect can be somewhat inhibiting: nakedness is a state of intrinsic vulnerability and most people feel more secure when not bathing in a space the size of a ballroom.

If you wish to make a more radical change and move the location of the bathroom, it is important to bear in mind that options can be somewhat limited by existing plumbing arrangements. In general it is easier to relocate a bathroom up or down a level, so that it connects into drainage at the same point, rather than shift it from the back to the front of your house, for example.

If the existing layout is excessively cramped, you might consider opting for smaller fittings. Sinks and baths come in a variety of sizes.

Allow enough room around each fixture or fitting. A sink, for example, needs to have some clear space on either side simply for elbow room.

In larger bathrooms, it is often a good idea to have a pair of sinks or washbasins so more than one person can use the room at the same time.

If there is sufficient floor area, a bathtub that is plumbed so that it is either free-standing or with only its head against a wall makes a much more attractive and dynamic arrangement than one which is confined in an alcove or set lengthways against a wall.

Converting a room into a bathroom can provide the opportunity to incorporate a dressing area.

FITTINGS AND FIXTURES

Choice of bathroom fittings and fixtures used to be
fairly restricted, with the principal variable being
colour. Today there is an enormous variety of styles
on the market. Taking inspiration from other cultures,
designers and architects have come up with radical
new fittings that redefine the whole bathroom: in
place of the claw-foot bath, there is the Japanese
hot tub in cedarwood; in place of the shower
cubicle, there is the minimal wet room with the
shower draining directly to an outlet in the floor.
Such innovative features are not for everyone – and

**Classic white porcelain sani-
taryware is unobtrusive and
long-lasting, both in terms of
style and of practicality.**

designer fittings come with designer price tags –
but the options for bathroom style have never been
greater. Visit a good bathroom showroom to make
a full investigation of the range available.

◻ If your preference is for standard fixtures and
fittings, avoid coloured suites, no matter how subtle
the shade. Coloured suites probably deter more
potential home buyers than any other interior
feature. Play safe and stick to white.

◻ Opt for the best quality you can afford.
Porcelain fittings are long lasting and easy to maintain in a pristine condition.

◻ Architectural salvage yards are a good source of
antique or traditional-style baths, sinks and lavatories, many of which are reclaimed from hotels
undergoing refurbishment.

◻ Many contemporary bathroom fittings are
demanding in terms of maintenance. Glass and
metal basins look spotty unless they are kept scrupu-
lously polished. Wooden hot tubs must be used
frequently or the wood will dry out and leak.

◻ You can give existing baths and sinks a new
lease of life by fitting new taps or shower sets in
chrome or brass. Bear in mind, however, that brass
taps need constant polishing or they will tarnish.

◻ If your bathroom is an unusual shape, oval or
corner baths make the best use of available space
and can be an attractive feature. Sunken baths are
the ultimate in luxury and sheer self-indulgence.

**Brightly coloured tiles in a
shower cubicle provide a
wake-up call. For maximum
effectiveness, showers may
need pumps to provide
adequate water pressure.**

BATHROOM STYLE

The bathroom offers considerable scope for creating an individual style: effects that might be overwhelming on a large scale are intriguing and characterful when the space is more confined.

Many bathroom themes take their cue from the elemental association with water. For a classical look, period fittings can be combined with tongue-and-groove panelling, marble-top vanity units and other details that are strong on architectural character. At the cutting edge of interior fashion, bathrooms and shower rooms are designed in a less structured way, displaying the evocative contrasts of materials such as stone, mosaic, glass or metal.

Whichever approach you adopt, it is important to remember that both the need for hygiene and high levels of humidity place certain practical constraints on your choices.

Etched blue glass used as a splashback (FAR LEFT) creates a suitably watery ambience. The strategically placed mirror (LEFT) is a tried and tested strategy for increasing the sense of space.

Linoleum tiles in a classic black and white check (RIGHT) are practical and good-looking.

SURFACES AND FINISHES

As in the kitchen, certain wall areas in the bathroom call for a greater degree of water-resistance than is offered by plasterwork. The areas immediately behind sinks and around bathtubs see more or less constant splashing and accordingly need protection; in the case of showers, that protection will have to be extended the full height of the surrounding walls. There are two approaches to adopt: one is to clad the wall in such a fashion that it blends in with the decorative scheme; the other is to make a feature of the change in material.

- Transparent materials such as toughened glass or acrylic sheets make inconspicuous splashbacks and surrounds.
- Sheet mirror can multiply the sense of space in a small bathroom. You may need professional help for installation; maintenance is also demanding.
- Use mirror tiles to enliven a plain wall.
- Tiling is the most common cladding option. Coordinate the colour of tiles with the rest of the wall for a seamless look or make a graphic contrast. Tiling is particularly attractive finished with a neat border of coving tiles or mosaic.

The tiny scale of mosaic sets up an interesting rhythm on bathroom surfaces. You can buy sheets of mosaic laid out in random patterns for a contemporary look or commission a mosaic artist to create a mural or individual design.

Many manufacturers market paint specially designed for the humid conditions of bathrooms.

If you want to paper areas of the bathroom, choose a vinyl-coated paper that is wipeable.

A grid of pristine mosaic tiles (LEFT) integrates bathroom fittings and introduces a subtle sense of pattern.

Natural fibre coverings can be used in bathroom areas (BELOW) provided they are not subject to regular soaking.

FITTED ELEMENTS

Bathrooms often look neater and more considered when individual features are united in a fitted scheme. Built-in bathrooms eliminate the awkward spaces under sinks and around lavatories that are difficult to clean and provide additional storage space for cleaning products and the like.

Wood is the most practical material for this application and can be varnished or painted to enhance water-resistance. Tongue-and-groove panelling has a refreshing simplicity; more elaborately detailed fitted units are available for those seeking to create a traditional look.

The tops of vanity units and the area around baths also provide the opportunity to ring the changes. Marble tops are supremely luxurious and distinctive; other types of stone, such as granite or slate, have a contemporary edge.

FLOORING

Softer flooring options, such as carpet and natural fibre coverings, are largely inadvisable in the bathroom as they have a tendency to rot when subject to constant humidity and moisture. Seagrass, which is a smooth water-repellent fibre, is a notable exception and can be used in circumstances where additional protection is provided around the bath.

■ Hard floors, such as those made of various types of stone slabs or tile, terrazzo, ceramic or terracotta tile score highly for practicality, good looks and water-resistance, but can become slippery when wet. Choose matt-textured rather than highly polished varieties; wooden decking beside the bath can provide a safer surface to step onto.

■ Wooden flooring is a sympathetic choice for the bathroom, provided it is not regularly soaked.

■ Plain painted floorboards have a pleasing simplicity and will resist spills.

■ Manmade or synthetic flooring options – including linoleum, rubber, cork and vinyl in sheet or tile formats – offer a wealth of choice, in terms of colour, design and overall aesthetic.

■ Vinyl flooring, the cheap and cheerful end of the market, often looks best in simple geometric patterns such as black and white squares.

LIGHTING

Water is an extremely efficient conductor of electricity and in areas such as the bathroom where there is the potential for the two to come in contact, the risks are high. Different safety legislation applies in different countries: consult a qualified electrician to make sure your proposals are safe. In the United States, for example, switches are grounded, which means they are safe to position in bathrooms. In Britain, on the other hand, lights must be controlled either by pull-cords or by switches positioned outside the bathroom door.

■ Fittings should be at least 2.5 metres (8ft) from showers, baths or sinks unless the bulb and the metal parts are completely enclosed.
■ Avoid pendant lights, table lamps and free-standing lamps.
■ Recessed downlights are ideal in the bathroom, both for reasons of safety and because of the fitted nature of the room.
■ Wall-mounted uplights create good background light, but do not use in proximity to showers or tubs.
■ Light mirrors to illuminate the face evenly. Flank

Daylight filtered by Venetian blinds and supplemented by strip lights to either side of the mirror (LEFT) provide ideal illumination for shaving or applying make-up. Downlights (RIGHT) are a practical choice for a bathroom, since layout and arrangement are fixed.

the mirror with a pair of tube lights or wall lights to avoid the type of heavy shadowing that comes from strong top lighting.

Striking effects can be achieved (at a price) with fibre optics. Fibre-optically lit showers or taps transform bathing into theatre.

Frosted glass in bathroom windows maintains privacy but maximises light. Otherwise, screen windows with louvred shutters, tailored or slatted blinds for flexible light control.

STORAGE

In the bathroom, as in other areas that are largely functional, storage and display tend to overlap somewhat. But while many bathroom accessories and products make attractive displays, if everything is out on view the result will have all the appeal of the personal care section of the supermarket. Some concealment, particularly for cleansers, supplies of toilet paper and other mundane necessities, makes practical and well as decorative good sense.

▨ Wall-mounted cabinets keep clutter away from sinks and bath surrounds.

▨ Containers such as wicker baskets or hampers and plastic or metal stacking boxes make flexible bathroom storage.

▨ If you have enough space, a free-standing armoire can be an attractive addition.

▨ Trolleys can be used as mobile containers for towels, flannels and bath products.

▨ Racks or caddies that hook over or bridge the sides of the bath are good places to keep soap, loofahs and flannels.

▨ Avoid open glass shelving immediately over sinks in case of breakages.

▨ Toothbrushes are best racked in a wall-mounted holder so that they can drain after use. Similarly, soaps need to be kept on a rack or a ridged or perforated dish.

▨ Hang up individual cosmetic bags, bathrobes or towels from a row of pegs or hooks.

▨ Keep emergency first aid supplies readily available in an unlocked container.

▨ Drugs and toxic cleaning products should be locked away or kept well out of children's reach.

A corner cupboard with open shelving above (LEFT) provides space to store both bathroom necessities and books to read in the bath. Individual perspex boxes housing a collection of mineral specimens (RIGHT) make an unusual display.

DISPLAY

Bathroom displays need not be very elaborate to be effective. Small touches, such as the odd picture, container of coloured soaps or decorative object contribute an important sense of vitality.

- Colour alone is an important decorative accent, especially if your fittings and fixtures are white. A row of coloured bottles backlit against a window provides visual pleasure when you are bathing.

- Decant lotions and potions into matching containers for a homogenous look.
- Small candles or nightlights around the bath provide instant atmosphere.
- Make use of free wall space to display a collection of framed pictures or prints.
- Fill large glass containers with shells or pebbles for a natural, elemental display.
- Certain types of plant, especially ferns, thrive in steamy bathroom atmospheres.

WORKROOMS

Our homes serve many functions these days, but increasingly they double up as places of work. One of the most significant changes brought about by the technological advances of recent years is the potential for work to be carried out almost anywhere: the modern office can be as minimal as a laptop and mobile phone. Accordingly, a growing number of people are seizing the opportunity to work at least part of the time from home.

The trend for home-working has added a new factor into the equation as far as interior arrangement and planning are concerned. The equipment required to carry out most types of desk job may be neat, portable and compact – and getting more so with each new computer generation – but that is not the end of the story. Finding the physical and psychological space to work effectively can prove a demanding exercise in spatial juggling.

The blurring of the boundaries between home life and working life often poses a strain on domestic arrangements simply because there is an in-built limit to the flexibility of most homes. The continuing popularity of the urban loft or converted 'live-work' space is just one indication of how difficult it can be to accommodate this new type of lifestyle within a more conventional framework. But with careful planning there are a number of solutions you can adopt. Which course of action you take will depend on the nature of your work and precisely how much of your professional life you expect to run from home. Many of the following points apply if you require space to pursue a serious hobby.

A leafy sunlit corner (LEFT) makes an ideal location. If you are running a business from home, a dedicated work room is essential (RIGHT).

ASSESSING YOUR NEEDS

'Working from home' is a term of some elasticity. If you intend to run a business from home, your requirements will necessarily be very different from someone who merely needs a quiet place to tackle paperwork from time to time. Noting the responses to these questions in your Notebook will help to clarify your particular requirements.

Does your work involve special equipment or pose any safety hazards?

How often do you work from home?

Occasionally, to take a break from office routine; whenever you need to catch up with deadlines; every evening and weekend?

Is your home business likely to expand? Will you need to employ others in the future?

Do you need meeting space? Do clients or work colleagues visit you at home?

Is the quality of natural light important?

Do you require access to phone/fax lines or ISDN lines?

Are other family members likely to be home while you are working?

PLANNING AND ARRANGEMENT

Serious professional ventures demand dedicated space; more intermittent home working can be slotted into the context of other areas in the home. Whichever choice you make, plan it out first with the Graph Paper and Templates.

MULTI-PURPOSE SPACES

You can set up an informal work area almost anywhere in the home. However, it is better to choose one place that offers optimum conditions in terms of natural lighting, access to phone lines and privacy, with the likelihood of minimal disruption, rather than drift about from location to location.

A settled home office, even if it is only a desk and filing cabinet, will provide a better basis for organisation. Furthermore, if work starts to invade absolutely every spare corner of your home, you will find it difficult to relax and get away from it.

Arrange the workspace so that there is an element of physical and psychological separation to enable you to concentrate. This can be as basic as placing a desk in a bay window or in front of a window, so that you turn your back on the rest of the room. Alternatively, some form of partition can be used to segregate the space: build a half-width wall to create a working alcove distinct from the other activities taking place in the same area.

Well-organised and well-lit workspace is an aid to concentration. Make sure that the worksurface is at the correct height and that your desk chair properly supports your back (LEFT). An attic studio, bathed in light (RIGHT), provides the ideal surroundings for creative inspiration.

SEPARATE WORKROOM

The truly 'spare' room is a fairly rare phenomenon in most households, but if you earn the bulk of your living from home it makes economic sense to fit out a permanent base where you can work entirely undisturbed behind a closed door, if necessary.

A separate study or office can enable you to function better professionally. Home-working takes a certain degree of discipline. If you are working in the kitchen, for example, distractions are ever-present – even washing up can seem an attractive proposition when a deadline looms. The mere act of crossing the threshold of your workroom can help you to put yourself in a different frame of mind, mentally prepared for a proper day's work. It also spells out the message to other family members that you are not constantly available. At the end of the day, you can leave work in progress, ready to be picked up again in the morning.

Many types of work do not require much floor space. Small bedrooms can make very efficient home offices, lined with shelves for files and reference material. There might also be room to include a sofabed for occasional overnight guests.

CONVERTED SPACES

Serious enterprises that you expect (or hope) will expand need a greater degree of separation from the daily activities of the household. This is particularly true if colleagues or clients need to visit you on a regular basis. A separate entrance not only minimises disruption, it also looks like you mean business. Garages, outbuildings or even sheds can be equipped to form efficient working environments at some distance from the household.

Basement and attic areas can often be usefully converted to workrooms. Of the two options, an office at the top of the house probably provides a more inspiring location than one that is underground. You may need planning permission for a loft conversion, particularly if you intend to include a roof window at the front of the house. Basements are more suitable for work involving machinery or semi-hazardous equipment or materials.

UTILITY ROOMS

Non-paid work of the routine domestic variety also merits a dedicated area, either a room or part of a room where you can locate the washing machine, dryer, ironing board, vacuum cleaner and related household cleaning products and accessories. Alternative locations include within kitchens or bathrooms or in basements.

A charmingly old-fashioned laundry room (FAR LEFT) takes the drudgery out of domestic chores.

If space is tight, a corner of a bedroom (LEFT) can do duty as a study area. A garden shed, converted into a home office (RIGHT), serves to minimise the possibility of distractions.

▶ NOTEBOOK

WORKROOM STYLE

There is no doubt that standard office equipment is eminently functional and generally fairly economical, particularly items acquired from secondhand or office surplus sources. However, a considerable advantage of working from home is the opportunity it provides to create a workspace that expresses your own personality and tastes rather than one that simply displays a bland corporate uniformity.

FURNISHING A WORKROOM

Desks come in a wide range of styles and price ranges, from elaborate antique roll-top affairs to plain laminate tops balanced on trestles.

Whichever you choose, make sure the basic physical parameters are covered.

■ The correct height for writing and other desk-bound paperwork is about 700mm (2ft 3in). The correct height for using a computer keyboard is about 5cm (2in) lower than this. You may require more than one worksurface.

■ Purpose-built computer workstations are widely available.

■ Although many traditional forms of desk were conceived at a time before the keyboard supplanted the fountain pen, they still provide an efficient means of organising correspondence.

A coat of white paint can soften the brutal appearance of office equipment (LEFT). A working wall of shelving (RIGHT) takes care of work-room storage requirements.

STORAGE

Unless you have a large dedicated workroom, it is unreasonable to expect to be able to store all your files and references within easy reach of your desk. Financial records and other material to which you no longer need to refer are best kept in a long-term storage area, such as an attic or basement.

▓ Well-secured metal shelving will be required if you are storing heavy or bulky items or equipment.

▓ Invest in matching document or box files to avoid an overly cluttered look.

▓ Choose cabinets in bright solid colours; alternatively stripped and polished metal finishes can be very attractive.

▓ Store back-up disks, CD Roms and other software in rigid plastic boxes or metal tins.

▓ Alternative storage containers include modular containers in plastic, wood, leather or cardboard.

▓ Store drawings or plans in plan chests, which have long shallow drawers, or individually rolled in plastic or cardboard tubes.

▓ Store small components such as nails, screws and fixings in a series of labelled jars or in divided containers, such as tackle boxes.

▓ Tools can be racked or hung on hooks from pegboards.

▓ Always keep potentially hazardous chemicals, paints, solvents and the like in a locked cupboard well out of the reach of children.

LIGHTING

Most types of work require a mixture of directional task lighting and a good overall level of background illumination.

░ Anglepoises and other forms of angled desk lamp are essential for desk work. Position the lamp so that light falls on the keyboard or page and does not shine in your eyes.

░ Uplighting is recommended for computer work, as it avoids the risk of reflections obscuring what is on the screen. Floor or table lamps are another good source of background lighting.

░ Don't neglect the impact of natural light. Angle computer screens away from direct light; you may also need to screen windows with Venetian blinds or semi-transparent curtains to reduce glare.

░ Ceiling-mounted fluorescent tubes make practical and economical solutions for utility rooms and workshops. If you require additional task lighting, a tube mounted on the wall or under a shelf behind a baffle will provide glare- and shadow-free illumination for working surfaces and areas where machines are used.

░ If your work is creative in any way and involves making fine colour judgments, north light is ideal (south light in the southern hemisphere). Daylight simulation bulbs, which are coloured blue, can also aid discrimination; alternatives are halogen lamps, which have true colour rendering.

HALLS, STAIRS
AND ENTRANCES

The connections from room to room, level to level and, most importantly, those places of transition between indoors and outdoors, have an impact out of all proportion to the actual volume of space they occupy or the amount of time you spend in them. What architects collectively call 'circulation space' – halls, stairs and entrances – are precisely that: spaces that we move through on our way somewhere else, rarely lingering longer than the time it takes to pick up the post from the mat or shrug off a coat. This, however, does not mean that they should be neglected, decoratively speaking. Well-presented circulation spaces send out a message of thoughtfulness and care.

The entrance has an obvious role to play as a point of welcome and crucially as a first impression that others will have of your home. But connecting areas are often visible from adjacent rooms and the views and vistas they provide can add an important sense of vitality and animation to the interior.

Such areas see a great deal of traffic and consequently suffer a significant degree of wear and tear. For obvious reasons, they should be safe places to negotiate and relatively easy places to maintain in a good condition. Safety is even more of an issue if you share your home with young children or an elderly relative.

An old-fashioned coat rack keeps outdoor gear hung neatly out of the way (LEFT). Touches of colour in the hall create a sense of welcome. A generous upper landing (RIGHT) provides a breathing space and the opportunity for display.

HALL, STAIR AND ENTRANCE STYLE

Halls, stairs and entrances may be the areas you see first and that provide the introduction to your home, but they should be considered in conjunction with other areas or you may limit your decorative options unnecessarily. If you intend to use a great deal of colour and pattern in the main living areas of your home, it can be a good idea to keep hallways neutral to act as a breathing space. The same strategy also works in reverse: vividly decorated hallways and stairs can provide a 'spine' of colour to link neutral or monochromatic living areas. Shades that might be a little tiring in larger doses are often very effective in connecting areas.

WALLS AND CEILINGS

Pattern can be very effective in hallways. In a stair-well, for example, a design with a strong vertical emphasis can serve to lead the eye upward, enhancing the sense of space. The disadvantage is that the lower portions of the wall can easily become marked and scuffed, especially if you are constantly bringing bikes in and out or if there are young children in the family. If you decide to paper a hallway, it can be a good idea to clad the lower third of the wall surface with a panelled dado for extra protection.

Vivid colour is often very effective in hallways and other connecting spaces, giving an instant uplift as you pass from area to area.

All types of stair carpeting must be securely anchored to prevent accidental tumbles. This open stairway, with its clean lines and minimal detailing (RIGHT), does not block light or interrupt views.

FLOORING

Entrances and stairways are areas where traffic is particularly heavy; safety and maintenance should be prime considerations.

Hard flooring is an obvious choice for entrances. Limestone and marble are elegant and refined; flag-stones and brick are more countrified. Ceramic tiles have a cool, modern look.

Black and white tiling is a traditional treatment for an entranceway. White marble with slate insets provides a touch of luxury; a similar effect can be achieved more economically with vinyl or linoleum.

Parquet, solid hardwood or wooden floorboards are practical and good-looking.

Any stair covering should be firmly secured to prevent accidents. Carpet can be close-laid or held in place with stair rods.

Stair carpeting should be very hard-wearing. Avoid thick or loopy pile varieties that can pose a hazard. Similarly, certain types of natural fibre covering, such as seagrass, thick coir and boucle weaves can be dangerous underfoot.

Runners in the form of flat-weave rugs such as dhurries or natural fibre mats can help to domesti-cate hard flooring in entrances and hallways.

Pay particular attention to the junctions between different types of flooring. Cover strips or neat seams prevent edges from lifting and tripping you up and look neat and well-considered.

Recessed lights mounted in the skirting boards create a glowing pathway. Downlights accentuate a display of fresh flowers in an alcove (RIGHT) and provide good general illumination for a curving hallway.

LIGHTING

Subtle and distinctive lighting emphasises the sense of welcome in entrances; at the same time, lighting should be sufficiently bright so that you can negotiate your way safely, particularly from level to level.

▨ If your hallway or staircase receives little in the way of direct natural light, think about installing a skylight to spill light down from level to level.

▨ A series of omni-directional ceiling lights, such as glass globes or paper lanterns, can be used to light a hallway. Avoid pendant fixtures that direct most of their light downward in a small circle.

▨ Wall-mounted sconces or uplights serve to bounce light off the ceiling and create a feeling of expansiveness.

▨ Avoid standard lamps or trailing flexes, which might prove a hazard.

▨ A small shaded lamp on a hall table makes an intimate focal point.

▨ Stairs can be lit by wall-mounted lights recessed at skirting board level.

▨ Don't forget to provide an external light over the front door so you do not approach your house in darkness. Lights that are triggered by heat or movement are excellent for security purposes.

▨ Landing or staircase windows do not have to be screened. Substitute clear glass with frosted, etched or stained panes for an evocative effect.

▨ Mirrors multiply the effects of light. Position a mirror opposite a doorway or window to set up views and vistas.

FURNISHING, FITTING AND DISPLAY

In general, circulation spaces should be kept as uncluttered as possible. Large pieces of furniture will devour floor space and serve to create unnecessary obstacles to movement. Hallways that are minimally furnished help to increase a sense of spaciousness.

If your hallway is large, a narrow table and a pair of hall chairs can be introduced. Such a grouping makes a natural punctuation point, or a place for messages to be left and post to be collected. A landing might accommodate a low chest or table that provides a surface for display.

Fresh flowers add vitality and a certain transient beauty to hallways (BELOW).

Halls can be fitted with cupboards and shelves to decant clutter from main living areas (RIGHT). A collection of baskets, colourful pitchers and jugs creates a cheerful welcome in a country cottage entrance (BELOW).

Wide hallways offer potential for fitted storage. A wall lined with bookshelves or built-in cupboards can house a great deal, easing pressure on adjacent areas. Similarly, the area underneath the stairs can be enclosed to provide additional storage space for outdoor gear and sports equipment. If your hallway is narrow, a row of hooks or pegs can provide a place to hang coats and hats.

If it is best to keep furnishing to a minimum, hallways do at least offer considerable potential for display.

A stairway or entrance can be treated as a picture gallery, with a collection grouped by theme or medium providing an intriguing backdrop.

A vase of fresh flowers on a console table, or a display of coloured glass arranged on a windowsill provide an uplifting accent of colour and interest.

PRACTICALITIES

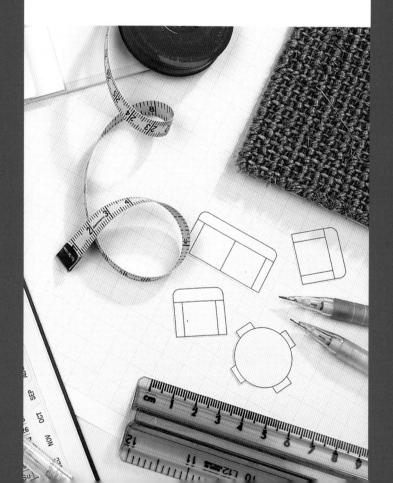

Whether you are shopping for a new sofa or an entire fitted kitchen, accurate planning is essential. The following section contains instructions on how to draw up scale plans on a sheet of graph paper. On pages 174–77 you will find a range of templates for common types of furniture and fittings – arranged room by room – that will enable you to make the most of your space and your budget.

▶ NOTEBOOK

The success of all forms of home improvement – including even the simplest redecoration job – depends on taking accurate measurements. You may not need to prepare a full-scale drawing of a room if you intend only to paint the walls and ceiling, but measuring is still important. If you don't have accurate measurements of the areas to be decorated, you are unlikely to buy the correct quantities of materials.

▨ Choose one system of measurement – imperial or metric – and stick to it at all costs.
▨ Invest in a good steel rule and enlist the help of a numerate friend or partner. Check your measurements several times.
▨ Think laterally. If you are buying a new sofa, don't just measure the space where you intend to put it: measure the width of doors, stairs and hall as well to ensure you can actually get the sofa into the room in the first place. Similarly, if you live in an apartment, check the width of the access stairs or service lift.

▶ GRAPH PAPER

A scale plan allows you to experiment on paper with different fitted layouts or furniture arrangements and forms the basis for more radical spatial decisions, such as removing partition walls, changing the position of doorways or adding a divider. Once again, good scale plans depend on accurate measurements and attention to detail.

▨ Begin by measuring the area or areas in question and draw a rough sketch, marking on the positions of windows, doors, fireplaces, alcoves or any other major architectural feature.
▨ Next, decide on a scale. For general living areas, such as living rooms, dining rooms and bedrooms, a scale of 1:50 is most useful. In practical terms this means that a line 2cm long on your plan represents 1 metre. (The imperial equivalent is ¼ in to 1 ft.) For more tightly planned spaces and ones in which there are fittings and fixtures to integrate such as kitchens and bathrooms, you may need to work on a larger scale, up to 1:20.
▨ Photocopy the graph paper on pages 78–79 and transfer your measurements to the copy using a sharp pencil and ruler.
▨ For complex decorative or design projects, you may need to mark on the position of power points and sockets, light fittings, radiators and other types of servicing.

▶ TEMPLATES

Templates of furniture and fittings allow you to try out different types of layout and arrangement quickly and painlessly. Although furniture and, to some extent, kitchen and bathroom fittings come in all shapes and sizes, there is a certain degree of standardisation. The templates included in the following pages cover most basic designs.

■ Templates must be to the same scale as your drawing. The templates in this section are 1:50.
■ Using drafting paper, trace round your chosen templates. Colour them in and cut them out. (Alternatively, make black and white photocopies of these pages and cut out the pieces you require.) Move the templates around on your scale plan to determine optimum arrangement.
■ Remember to include free areas around furniture and fittings to allow for access. A double bed may fit an alcove exactly, but bedmaking will be difficult without some room to manoeuvre. In the same way, allow enough room for cupboard doors to swing open or for bending down to retrieve objects from lower shelves.
■ For a more concrete picture, you can draw full-size templates onto sheets of lining paper and place them in the area in question.

TO DIY OR NOT TO DIY

Careful planning is within the capabilities of most people. From that point on, however, it is a different story. Executing a decorative scheme – painting, papering, tiling, putting up curtains or shelves – can involve a wide range of skills. Before you get busy with the paintbrush or powerdrill, think carefully about how much of the work you are really qualified or prepared to undertake. If you are pressed for time, inexperienced or simply impetuous, call in the professionals – it will save money in the long run and you will get a much better result. Whatever you intend to do, the following are jobs for the experts.

■ Floor laying. Flooring materials tend to be bulky and unwieldy and are sometimes heavy. Special fixatives may be required.
■ Replastering or substantial making good. Really poor wall or ceiling surfaces require professional help. Do not be tempted to paint or paper over a rough surface without proper preparation beforehand. You'll simply be wasting your time.
■ Any alteration to services, such as electricity, drainage, heating and fixed lighting arrangements.
■ Alterations to the structure or fabric of your home, such as moving walls, windows or entrances.
■ In general, any jobs that involve specialist equipment, such as floor sanders. While many tools are available for hire from special outlets, you should exercise great caution before attempting to do the work yourself.

LIVING ROOMS

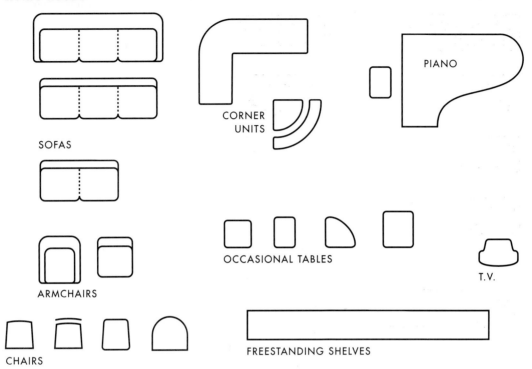

SOFAS

CORNER UNITS

PIANO

ARMCHAIRS

OCCASIONAL TABLES

T.V.

CHAIRS

FREESTANDING SHELVES

DINING AREAS

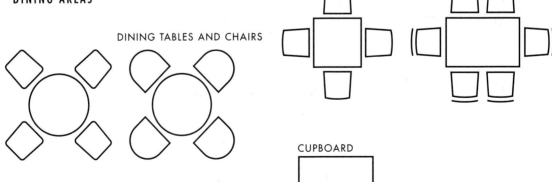

DINING TABLES AND CHAIRS

CUPBOARD

KITCHENS

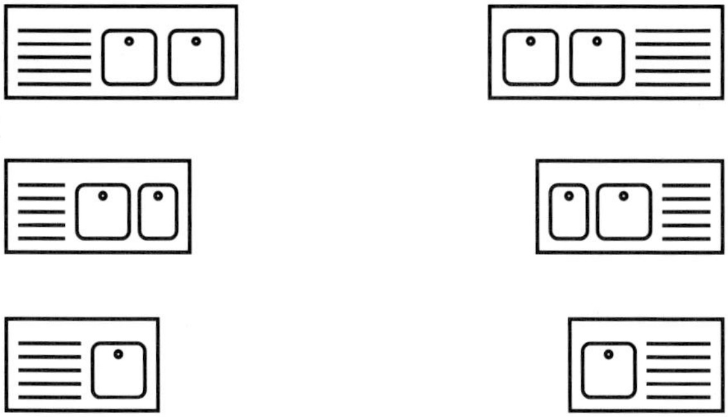

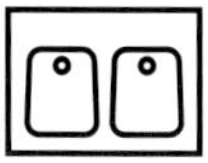

SINK AND
DRAINER UNITS

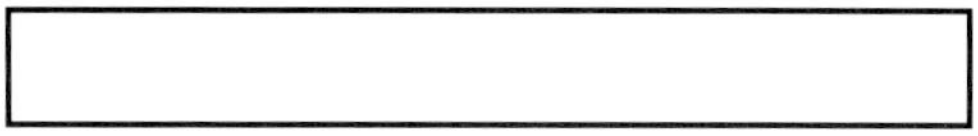

SHELF UNITS

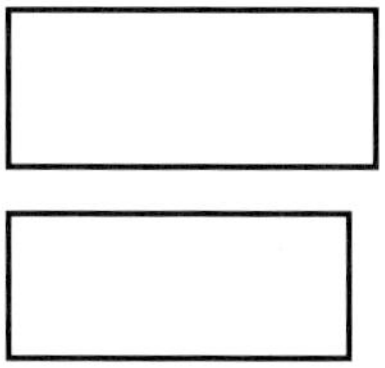

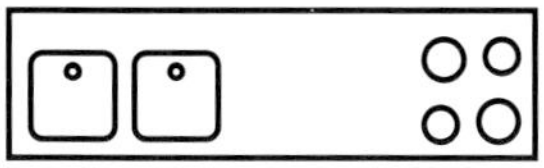

STOVES

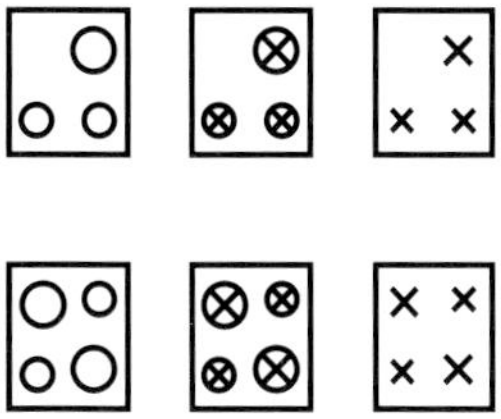

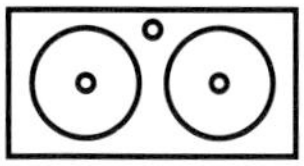

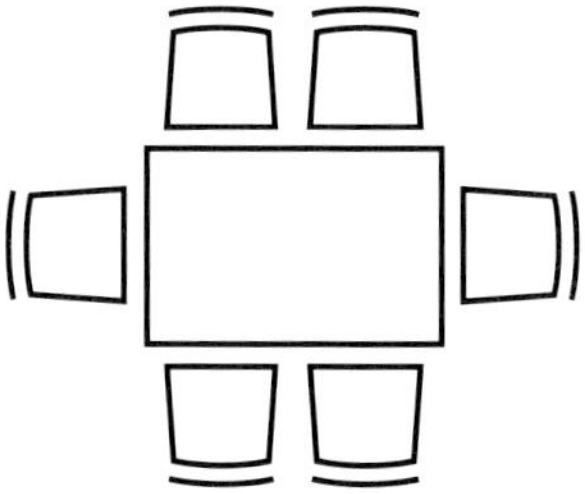

KITCHEN TABLES AND CHAIRS

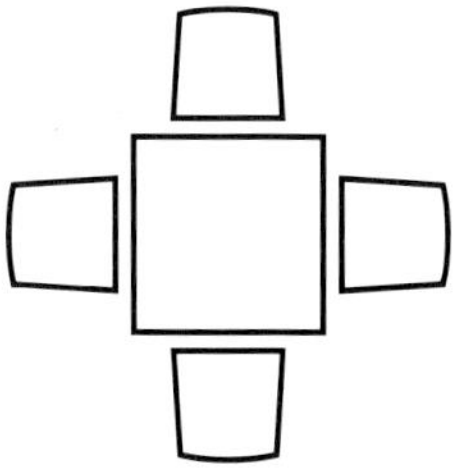

BEDROOMS

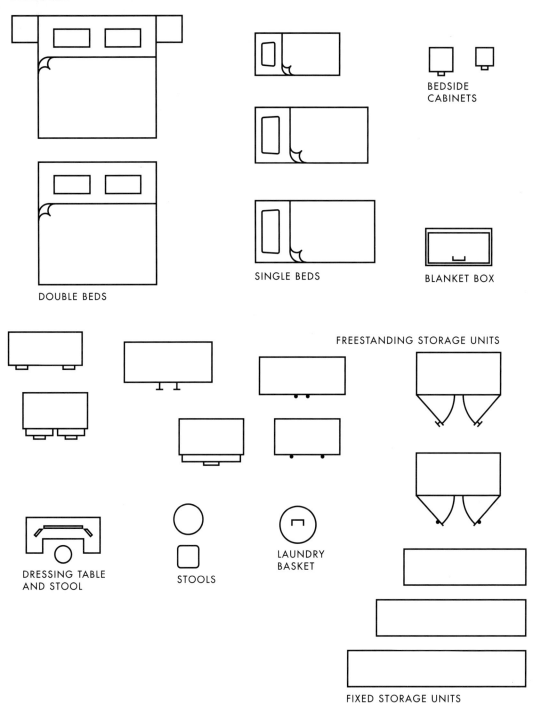

BEDSIDE
CABINETS

SINGLE BEDS

BLANKET BOX

DOUBLE BEDS

FREESTANDING STORAGE UNITS

DRESSING TABLE
AND STOOL

STOOLS

LAUNDRY
BASKET

FIXED STORAGE UNITS

BATHROOMS

BATHS

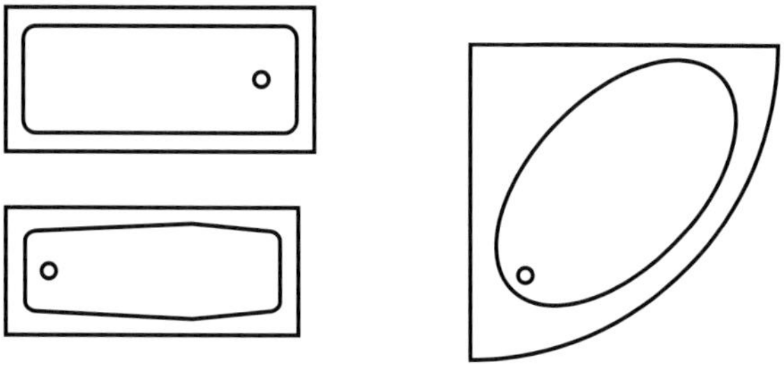

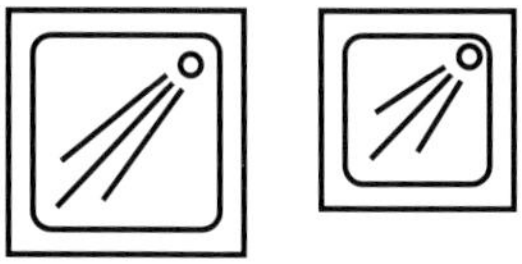

WASH BASINS

SHOWERS

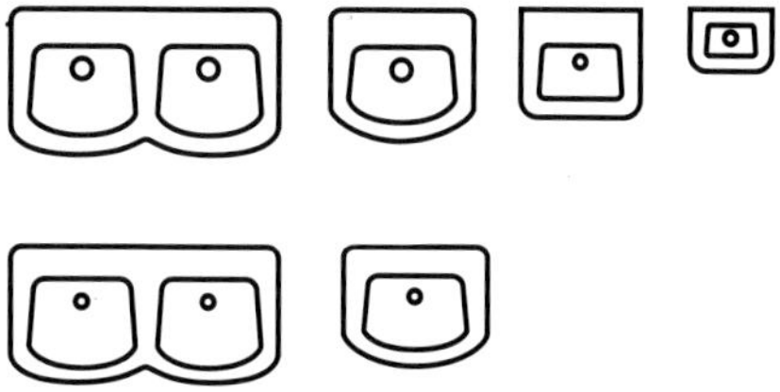

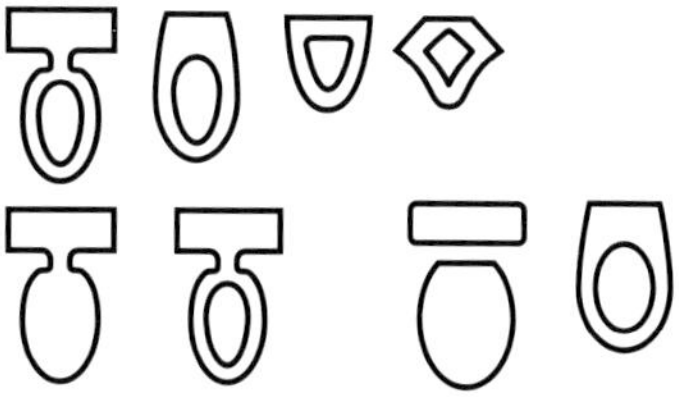

LAVATORIES

WORKROOMS

TABLES

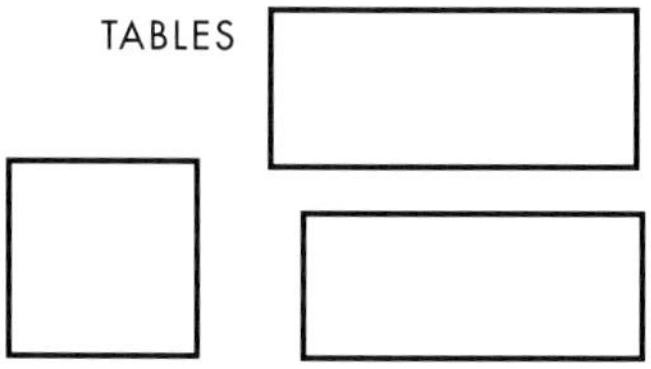

CHAIRS

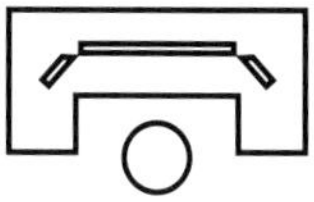

DESK AND STOOL

HALLS

OCCASIONAL TABLES

CHAIRS

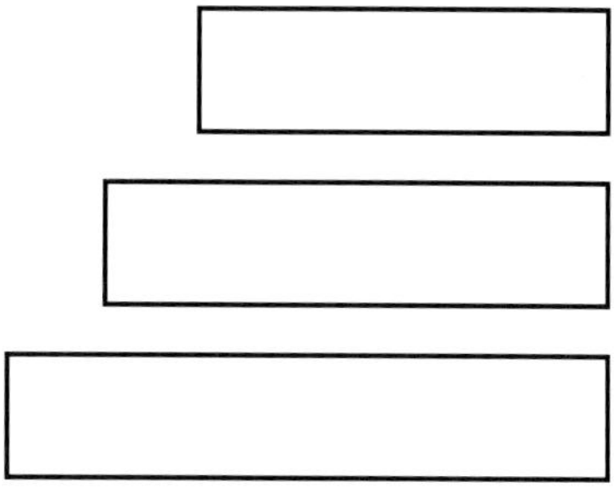

STORAGE UNITS

1 SQUARE = 50cm

INDEX

CREDITS

Breslich & Foss would like to thank the following individuals and agencies for permission to reproduce images in the book:

7 Camera Press/*Schöner Wohnen*; 12 View/Richard Glover; 13 Narratives/Polly Wreford; 14 Camera Press/*Familie & Co*; 15 View/Chris Gascoigne; 17 José King/ARK Architects & Designers; 18 (above) Richard Glover; (below) José King/architect Femi Santos; 19 José King/architects Luigi Beltrandi & Mya Nanakides; 27 Ray Main/Mainstream/designer Fleur Rossdale; 28 (left) Narratives/Polly Wreford; (right) Narratives/Jan Baldwin; 29 (left) Ray Main/Mainstream; (right) Mark Luscombe-Whyte/www.elizabethwhiting.com; 30 Lu Jeffery/www.elizabethwhiting.com; 31 Narratives/Jan Baldwin; 33 Paul Ryan/International Interiors/designers Haskins & Page; 36 Paul Ryan/International Interiors/designer Frances Halliday; 37 Narratives/Jan Baldwin; 38 Narratives/Polly Wreford; 39 Tom Leighton/www.elizabeth-whiting.com; 41 Narratives/Polly Wreford; 43 Camera Press/*Schöner Wohnen*; 44 Narratives/Jan Baldwin; 46 left Paul Ryan/International Interiors/architect Jacob Cronstedt; 46 right Ray Main/Mainstream/designer Fleur Rossdale; 47 Paul Ryan/International Interiors/designers Kay Moskal & Ken Foreman; 48 Paul Ryan/International Interiors/designer Jo Nahem; 48–49 Ray Main/Mainstream/architect Spencer Fung; 49 Camera Press/*Zuhause Wohnen*; 50 Mark Luscombe-Whyte/www.elizabethwhiting.com; 51 Ray Main/Mainstream; 52 (left) The Interior Archive/Ken Hayden/designer Jonathan Reed; right José King/ARK Architects & Designers; 53 The Interior Archive/Edina van der Wyck/florist Stephen Woodhams; 54 Red Cover/Mark Bolton; 55 (left) José King/architect Damien Darcy; (right) Paul Ryan/International Interiors/designers Kastrup & Sjunnesson; 56–57 View/Peter Cook; 58 Ray Main/Mainstream; 59 Ray Main/Mainstream; 60–61 José King/architect Guy Stansfeld; 63 José King/Peter Tigg Partnership Architects; 65 José King/Peter Tigg Partnership Architects; 70–71 View/Peter Cook; 72 Ray Main/Mainstream/designer Vincente Wolfe; 73 Narratives/Polly Wreford; 74 Camera Press/*Zuhause Wohnen*; 75 Paul Ryan/International Interiors/designers Pavel Kapic & Alyssia Lazan; 76 (left) The Interior Archive/Edina van der Wyck; (right) Paul Ryan/International Interiors/designer John Saladino; 77 (left) Paul Ryan/International Interiors/designers Kay Moskal & Ken Foreman; (right) The Interior Archive/Edina van der Wyck; 78 Ray Main/Mainstream; 79 Tim Street-Porter/www.elizabethwhiting.com; 80 The Interior Archive/Simon Upton; 81 Red Cover/Ken Hayden; 82 Paul Ryan/International Interiors/designer Sharone Einhorn; 83 Houses & Interiors/Jake Fitzjones; 84 Camera Press/*Sarie Visi*/Ryno/Lynette Monsson; 85 Di Lewis/www.elizabethwhiting.com; 86 The Interior Archive/Edina van der Wyck/florist Stephen Woodhams; 87 Paul Ryan/International Interiors/designers Kastrup & Sjunnesson; 88 Paul Ryan/International Interiors/designer Frances Halliday; 89 Dennis Krukowski/Glenn Gissler Design; 90 Houses & Interiors/Steve Hawkins & Teresa Ward; 91 Paul Ryan/International Interiors/designer Sharone Einhorn; 92 Paul Ryan/International Interiors/designer Bernardo Urquita; 93 Dennis Krukowski/David Webster and Associates; 94 The Interior Archive/Simon Upton; 95 The Interior Archive/Henry Wilson/designer Nick McMahon; 96 Paul Ryan/International Interiors/architect Jacob Cronstedt; 97 left The Interior Archive/Edina van der Wyck; 97 right Paul Ryan/International Interiors/designer Vincente Wolf; 98 Narratives/Peter Dixon; 99 Paul Ryan/International Interiors/designer Victoria Hagen; 100 Paul Ryan/International Interiors/designers Kastrup & Sjunnesson; 101 left Paul Ryan/International Interiors/designer Kriistina Ratia; 101 right Di Lewis/www.elizabethwhiting.com; 102 Red Cover/Christopher Drake; 103 Paul Ryan/International Interiors/designer Mary Foley; 104 Ray Main/Mainstream; 105 Houses & Interiors/Jake Fitzjones/Alan Power Architects; 106 The Interior Archive/Andrew Wood/designer Christine

Rucker; 107 Paul Ryan/International Interiors/architects MC2 Design; 108 Red Cover/Brian Harrison; 109 José King/architect Guy Stansfeld; 110 Paul Ryan/International Interiors/designer Jan des Bouvrie; 111 above Red Cover/Winfried Heinze; 111 below The Interior Archive/Henry Wilson/designer Nick McMahon; 112 The Interior Archive/Simon Upton; 113 Red Cover/Christopher Drake; 114 Dennis Krukowski/Florence Perchuk C.K.D.; 115 left Tim Street-Porter/www.elizabethwhiting.com; 115 right Houses & Interiors/Jake Fitzjones 116 above Ray Main/Mainstream/Babylon Design; 116 below David Giles/www.elizabethwhiting.com; 117 The Interior Archive/Edina van der Wyck/florist Stephen Woodhams; 118 The Interior Archive/Andrew Wood/designer Kate Bler; 119 Ray Main/Mainstream; 120 The Interior Archive/Andrew Wood; 120-121 Paul Ryan/International Interiors/designer Kastrup & Sjunnesson; 122 The Interior Archive/Andrew Wood; 123 José King/ARK Architects & Designers; 125 The Interior Archive/Andrew Wood/designer Christine Rucker/The White Company; 126 The Interior Archive/Andrew Wood/architect Spencer Fung; 127 Paul Ryan/International Interiors/designer Sharone Einhorn; 128 Paul Ryan/International Interiors/architect David Lung; 129 The Interior Archive/Edina van der Wyck/designer Atlanta Bartlett; 130 Richard Glover/Maria Duff Design; 131 Paul Ryan/International Interiors/designers Kastrup & Sjunnesson; 132 Red Cover/Brian Harrison; 133 Ray Main/Mainstream; 134 right Ray Main/Mainstream/designer John Minshaw; 135 Ray Main/Mainstream; 136 Paul Ryan/International Interiors/designer Francis Halliday; 137 Houses & Interiors/Gwenan Murphy; 138 left The Interior Archive/Edina van der Wyck/architect Josh Schweitzer; 138 right Paul Ryan/International Interiors/designer Mary Foley; 139 Paul Ryan/International Interiors/designer John Michael Ekeblad; 140 Paul Ryan/International Interiors/designer Sabina Streeter; 141 Ray Main/Mainstream; 142 José King/architect Guy Stansfeld; 143 The Interior Archive/Andrew Wood/designer Christine Rucker/The White Company; 144 Red Cover/Christopher Drake; 144-145 Houses & Interiors/Roger Brooks; 146 left Houses & Interiors/Jake Fitzjones/designer Dale Loth Architects; 146 right Ray Main/Mainstream; 147 Paul Ryan/International Interiors/designer Mary Foley; 148 José King/ARK Architects & Designers; 148-149 The Interior Archive/Simon Upton/designer Bill Amberg; 150 The Interior Archive/Ken Hayden/designer Jonathan Reed; 151-152 Ray Main/Mainstream; 153 José King/architect Guy Stansfeld; 154 The Interior Archive/Andrew Wood/designer Peter Wylly/Babylon Design; 155 Spike Powell/ww.elizabethwhiting.com; 156 Camera Press/*Neues Wohnen*; 156 EWA/www.elizabethwhiting.com; 158 left The Interior Archive/Tim Beddow; 158 right The Interior Archive/Edina van der Wyck/architect Josh Schweitzer; 159 Di Lewis/www.elizabethwhiting.com; 160 The Interior Archive/Edina van der Wyck/designer Atlanta Bartlett; 161 Julian Nieman/www.elizabethwhiting.com; 162 Narratives/Jan Baldwin; 163 Paul Ryan/International Interiors/designers Kristina & Bjorn Sahlqvist; 164 Paul Ryan/International Interiors/designer Jo Nahem; 165 left Narratives/Jan Baldwin; 165 right Ray Main/Mainstream/architect Simon Condor; 166 The Interior Archive/Ken Hayden/designer Jonathan Reed; 167 José King/architect Damien Drarcy; 168 The Interior Archive/Andrew Wood/designer Leonie Lee Whittle/Snap Dragon; 168 above José King/ARK Architects & Designers; 169 below Di Lewis/www.elizabethwhiting.com.

© Breslich & Foss (Shona Wood): 1, 3, 4–5, 8, 11, 20, 22, 23, 24, 34, 35, 42, 45, 66–67, 69, 171.

With thanks to 'And So to Bed': 30 (right), 40, 124, 134 (left).

Project manager JANET RAVENSCROFT
Designer JANE FORSTER
Templates ANTHONY DUKE
Illustrations TERRY EVANS
Index PETER BARBER